GUARDING YOUR JOY

Strength to survive the storms of life

Kwaku S. Darkwa - MD

GUARDING YOUR JOY

Copyright © 2018 by Kwaku S. Darkwa – MD

All rights reserved. No part of this book may be used, reproduced, stored in a retrieval system or transmitted, in any form or by any means, including mechanical, electronic, photocopy, recording, scanning and methods not invented or in common use at the time of this publication, without the prior written permission of the publisher.

Published by Vike Springs Publishing Ltd. – London, UK
Contact: **admin@vikesprings.com**
Website: **www.vikesprings.com**

First Edition
ISBN-13: 978-1-9998509-2-0 - E-book
ISBN-13: 978-1-9998509-3-7 - Paperback

Printed in the United Kingdom
and the United States of America
Cover image: istock.com/molchanovdmitry

To request Dr Darkwa for speaking engagements or interviews, please send an email to: sapondarkwa@yahoo.com

Dr Darkwa's books are available at special discounts when purchased in bulk for promotions or as donations for educational, inspirational and training purposes.

Limit of Liability/Disclaimer of Warranty

This publication is designed to provide accurate and authoritative information in regard to the subject matter covered. It is sold with the understanding that the publisher and author are not engaged in rendering physiological, financial, legal or other licensed services. The publisher and the author make no representations or warranties with respect to the completeness of the contents of this work. If expert assistance or counselling is needed, the services of a specific professional should be sought. Neither the publisher nor the author shall be liable for damages arising here from. The fact that an organization or website is referred to in this work as a citation and/or a potential source of further information does not mean that the author or the publisher endorses the information that the organization or website may provide or recommendations it may make, nor does the cited organization endorse affiliation of any sort to this publication. Also, readers should be aware that due to the ever-changing information from the web, Internet websites and URLs listed in this work may have changed or been removed.

All trademarks or names referenced in this book are the property of their respective owners, and the publisher and author are not associated with any product or vendor mentioned.

CONTENTS

DEDICATION	vii
ACKNOWLEDGMENT	ix
INTRODUCTION	xiii
THE DEPOSIT OF JOY	1
PREVAILING JOY	11
JOY UNDER FIRE	21
WHEN NOTHING WORKS	39
GOD IS NOT ASLEEP - LOOK FOR HIM	47
DO NOT THROW HOPE OUT	59
ESSENTIAL REMEMBRANCE	69
WHEN FRIENDS FAIL US	75
EXCESSIVE MOURNING	87
LIFT UP YOUR DEFENCES	95
GOD IS JUDGE	113

DEDICATION

To Stella, my dear wife
The journey has been tough, but God
has been so good to us.

ACKNOWLEDGMENT

Many thanks to Elizabeth Akutsa for working on this manuscript. To God the gracious father and creator of the universe, I cannot say thank you enough for the gift of life, health, and strength. To my daughters Juanita and Michelle, you are a great inspiration in the midst of all life's challenges.

Father, to Thee we look in all our sorrow,
Thou art the fountain whence our healing flows;
Dark though the night, joy cometh with the morrow;
Safely they rest who on Thy love repose.

When fond hopes fail and skies are dark before us,
When the vain cares that vex our lives increase,
Comes with its calm the thought that Thou art o'er us,
And we grow quiet, folded in Thy peace.

Naught shall affright us, on Thy goodness leaning;
Low in the heart faith singeth still her song;
Chastened by pain we learn life's deeper meaning,
And in our weakness Thou dost make us strong.

Patient, O heart, though heavy be Thy sorrows;
Be not cast down, disquieted in vain;
Yet shalt thou praise Him, when these darkened furrows,
Where now He plougheth, wave with golden grain.

— **Frederick Lucian Hosmer**

INTRODUCTION

Guarding Your Joy is a very inspirational book. Seldom is an entire book devoted to the subject of joy. Rather, joy appears as an aspect or a fraction of a book. How important is the subject of joy today? In most lives, joy is almost absent. For most people who are struggling in their walk with God assume that most of God's blessings, including joy, belong to a privileged few — but they are excluded.

There are many Christians whose lives are virtually drained of joy. This is toxic and a fatal life condition! The demands of school, job, family, relationships, health and economic challenges, the need to make ends meet, the stress of work, and the absence of answers or people to confide in have conspired together and driven many lives to the edge of despair. Once, David lifted up his eyes to the hills, and his challenge was where to find help. He concluded that help cannot come from the hills, where his gaze was, or from any man, but only from the Lord, the Maker of heaven and earth.

There is help for the child of God. He/she has answers for every challenge. Joy is key for opening the floodgates to physical and emotional healings, restoration, and much more. This makes this book a must-read for every individual and family. Each chapter has something unique to offer on this theme — from the source of joy, the fact that Satan wants to steal your joy, the conditions that can take your joy away, and the need to safeguard it with all the grace given to you. Your joy can ward off many spiritual ills, physical ills, as well as emotional-health conditions and give you a healthy attitude, a sound body, and a prolonged life here on earth.

After you have digested the content of this book, you will know that joy is not a mere feeling of temporal excitement or happiness but a lifelong divine gift. It is a blessing from God to you. Like any other blessing, joy needs to be protected or secured through serious, personal responsibility. The things you allow to enter your mind can affect your emotions and consequently derail your life. Among the people who have greater influence on you are family and friends. People you have intimate relations with contribute to the state of your joy. Because of this, you have a duty to ensure that your joy lasts.

Dr. Kwaku Darkwa has also provided some activities or measures for re-establishing your joy even if you have lost it. Having your joy restored is as important as having your very life back. However, what is required is sincerity to oneself. Is something missing in your life? If yes, what is it? Are you just enduring each day of your life? Is it drained of the magic, passion, and glow? Are you sick and tired of your work and the people you relate with? Has your challenge a name? If most of your answers are in the affirmative, then this book is yours.

The truth is, God wants you to have His joy in its fullness. If you have lost the spark in your life, it is not too late. Keep on reading the chapters of this book, which is the first part of a series of 3 on this subject. May you find answers and strength to deal with your challenges in the pages of Guarding Your Joy. When you are done, please pass the book on. God bless you.

Chapter 1
THE DEPOSIT OF JOY

> *Keep your heart with all vigilance, for from it flow the springs of life.*
> **Proverbs 4:23**

We were created as creatures of joy. In fact, the Good Book tells us that God rejoiced over His creation, and this includes you and me. You have bundled within you a great deposit of a valuable commodity called "joy." God created man from the dust of the earth, formed man's feet, toes, legs, torso, and hands with fingers, and then fixed a neck, upon which He placed the human head. Then His perfect eyes inched up from the toes of your feet and slowly but surely scrutinized every part of your formed body. When He was pleased with all He saw, then He released the breath of life into the original man's nostrils, flowing into his chest and then into his entire body. Within that warm force of His breath was a multidimensional treasure that transformed the clay into a living soul.

When the first man came alive, I believe he stretched out his hands as if he had been in a deep sleep, and something began to glow from within him. This glow drew the attention of the elements of the entire universe to him. It made him feel at peace with himself and in harmony with all creation. Joy was a vital force of this inner treasure. It helped him to identify with his creator. Man rejoiced at being part of a sinless earth, and the vast universe and all created beings, including the angels, sang in joy. Joy kept man in harmony with his earthly body and system.

> *"If the sight of the blue skies fills you with joy, if a blade of grass springing up in the fields has power to move you, if the simple things in nature have a message you understand, rejoice, for your soul is alive."*
> **Eleanor Duse**

Joy helps you harmonize with all the things you see and find around you. Nature appreciated brings joy to your heart, and it takes a measure of joy within you to appreciate nature. Nature has an amazing effect on the human spirit and soul, and you cannot experience true peace and joy when there is chaos within you. If you want to enjoy peace and joy on this side of the universe, you need to appreciate and respect the universe you have been born into. The beauty of nature brings joy into your heart as well. It is not a coincidence that, when you lose your joy, God can use nature to communicate to you and to heal your wounded soul. Even in your depressed mood, attention to greenery, mountains and valleys, or the waves of the sea upon the shore can give a boost to your spirit.

> *"I go to nature to be soothed and healed, and to have my senses put in order."*
> **John Burroughs**

God gave you eyes to see the beauty of nature and a heart to appreciate His created genius in and around you.

In all your interactions with everything you find around you, you as a social being will be ineffective in your interactions without the force of joy. Human interaction is vital for human existence, and human existence is compromised when you lose your joy. It occupies a place in your heart which nothing else can replace, and, without it, men walk this earth as incomplete and unfulfilled beings. God had no other place to hide this great deposit in the entire universe other than in the heart of a man. God expects you to jealously guard this deposit of joy and every other deposit He has bequeathed to you.

Why the Heart?

The true essence of mankind is the spirit man. You are a spiritual being first and foremost and not a physical being. Man is a spirit being having an earthly experience and not the reverse. The physical is just a wrapper covering the true man — the spirit. You are indeed a spirit being who possesses a soul and dwells in a physical body. God in His wisdom breathes the breath of life into man's spirit. This is where the treasure deposit is located. The body has become a poor container to store a treasure. In fact, the reason you have a body is because you cannot exist in this earthly realm and experience this realm without it. That is why all mortals in this earthly sphere have bodies.

The body of man, after the Fall, has become weak as a container, such that any small harm to the body predisposes the spirit to depart or leave the body. The body has an integument, or skin, to prevent outside agents from entering it. Simple bacteria can compromise the spirit's residence here on earth. The body has also become a poor residence for the soul of man. The soul of man, which comprises the mind, the will, and emotions, can easily be influenced by what happens to the physical body.

Everything affecting the human body and the soul can eventually compromise the deposit within his heart. Guarding against all such agents that can cause harm is to love your very essence and every deposit God has placed in you. Sickness, pain, worry, fear, hunger, poverty and other negative factors can affect the deposit of joy within if you allow them entry into your heart.

Keep your heart with all vigilance, for from it flow the springs of life.
Proverbs 4:23

You were created and conditioned to exhibit and operate at your fullest potential in an atmosphere of joy. You were made to love God, the Creator of all men and all created things, and desire His presence, in which is the very vital force of life and joy. In this environment, you will have and experience one form of heavenly pleasure after another. The unfolding of God's blessings in your life has everything to do with a heart at rest and joyful in his Maker and Creator.

You make known to me the path of life; in your presence there is fullness of joy; at your right hand are pleasures forevermore.
Psalm 16:11

Even as you enjoy the unraveling of God's gracious love and gifts here on this finite earth, your ability to fully enjoy and partake in what He has lavishly granted to you is enabled by the joy of God. Your vision and perception are compromised when this joy is lacking or absent. God has already blessed you with blessings of the heavens above and blessings of the earth beneath. He has blessed you with the blessings of the mountains and the blessings of the valley.

God has bequeathed to you the peace of the gentle, flowing springs and the wonders and amazements of mighty waterfalls. The beauty of the changing patterns of the morning, afternoon, and evening sky is for you to behold. The intrigue that follows tiny creatures like the ants, the science that allows the bees to fly, and several other of nature's blessings have been given to man. However, a lack of God's presence and joy can convert this beautiful cosmos into a very mundane and even a hopeless place to live.

The joy of the LORD enthrones mankind and enables him to relate to God and man rightly. It enables you to trust in God and in your fellow man. In the joy of the LORD is stability, hope, trust, longevity, health, prosperity, assurance, and every other good thing God has blessed you with. It keeps several other blessings together. It enables you to experience and enjoy the strength and the other provisions of God.

The Place of Joy in the Equation of Life

I believe King David was able to accomplish all he did for God because he understood the place of joy in the equation of life. God was pleased with him because his heart was right. David would not allow the vicissitudes of life to kill his joy and put him down and out. He was able to draw strength from God when he needed it most. He was able to ascend the throne eventually, even though the journey to the throne was punctuated with pain, frustration, doubts, uncertainties, betrayals, loneliness, rejection, and gloom. How did he do this? I believe the joy of the LORD was his strength.

David had many desires as a young man, but many of them looked too bleak to materialize. He had brothers, most likely stepbrothers, who did not really like him. He had a father who was somehow so detached from his life that he forgot David even existed. He spent lonely days and dreary nights on the open fields and in the wilderness with the family sheep. He faced the dangers of beasts in the field, and it is documented that he had wrestled with a lion and a bear just to ensure that the number of sheep would not fall short. How was he able to go through all these pressures? His heart was right, and the joy of the LORD gave him strength.

When he eventually ascended the throne of Israel, life was not as easy and pleasant as he would have wanted. I believe many were not happy with him. It took years for his people to accept him as king. There were people with disloyal hearts around. He had never been king before, and all he had managed before were a few, probably miserable, sheep. How was he able to deal with the uncertainties of the initial years of kingship and the great responsibility of governing a people who were not united? The joy of the LORD was his strength. The joy of the LORD enabled him to look beyond his present state and inadequacies and to depend on the strength that flowed towards him from the assurance he had that God was with him.

This enabled David to be granted the desires of his heart. It empowered him to believe that he would have his prayers answered by God. It broadened his horizon to receive great blessings from God. It promoted David at every level, and he was happy with his blessings at every level of his life's journey. It secured his crown upon his head and granted him length of days. It empowered him for battle and shifted the battles into the arena of God. It moved God to take over David's battles and granted him one sweet victory after another. No wonder his throne is an everlasting throne, as God promised him a dynasty that is unending.

O LORD, in your strength the king rejoices, and in your salvation how greatly he exults! You have given him his heart's desire and have not withheld the request of his lips.

For you meet him with rich blessings; you set a crown upon his head. He asked life of you; you gave it to him, length of days forever and ever. His glory is great through your salvation; splendor and majesty you bestow on him.

For you make him most blessed forever; you make him glad with the joy of your presence. For the king trusts in the LORD, and through the steadfast love of the Most High he shall not be moved.

Your hand will find out all your enemies; your right hand will find out those who hate you. You will make them as a blazing oven when you appear. The LORD will swallow them up in his wrath, and fire will consume them.

You will destroy their descendants from the earth, and their offspring from among the children of man. Though they plan evil against you, though they devise mischief, they will not succeed.

For you will put them to flight; you will aim at their faces with your bows. Be exalted, O LORD, in your strength! We will sing and praise your power.

Psalm 21

Chapter 2
PREVAILING JOY

Joy Appreciates God's Gracious Provisions

It is a great blessing to live and an even greater blessing to enjoy the life God so generously grants you. The joy of the Lord is what enables you to enjoy the life He has given you and to use everything He enables you to have in this life.

> *Go, eat your bread with joy, and drink your wine with a merry heart, for God has already approved what you do. Let your garments be always white. Let not oil be lacking on your head. Enjoy life with the wife whom you love, all the days of your vain life that he has given you under the sun, because that is your portion in life and in your toil under the sun. Whatever your hands find to do, do it with your might, for there is no work or thought or knowledge or wisdom in Shoel, to which you are going.*
> **Ecclesiastes 9:7-10**

The great philosopher Solomon had these words of wisdom for you. Put your heart into whatever endeavour you find yourself engaged in on this earth. Enjoy your meals even though they may not be the best and most appetizing. Wear the few clothes you have with joy and pride even if they are not new. Love your wife and stop fantasizing about life with some other woman. Life is short, and you need to make the best of your time here. Live daily with gladness and appreciation for the little you have. Do not compare your life with others and what they may have that you do not have. Embrace your life, your position, your job, your friends, and your relationships with joy.

Many times, this seems so elusive, as you are prone to desire and admire what other people have and you don't. Your eyes appreciate what belongs to others, hence, you are deprived of the power to look and see your own blessings. How can you appreciate having little when you are bombarded daily with what the world calls "the enviable standard of success": worldly achievements, pride, and the amassing of material things on this side of the universe? If you seek joy, you will not find it without helping others enjoy the same. In the midst of all the trouble around you, you can find happiness if you consider others above your selfish wants.

> *"The best way to cheer yourself up is to try to cheer somebody else up."*
> **Mark Twain**

It is the joy of God that enables you to eat your food in gladness and to drink your wine with a joyful heart. It is the joy of the Lord that enables you to enjoy life, to find gladness even in the hand-me-down clothing you wear, and to always anoint your head with oil to brighten your face, in spite of all the challenges you may be going through. His joy enables you to enjoy all that He graciously supplies. You need to live with an appreciation of the graciousness and provision of a bigger hand. There is a God, and He is gracious to all who seek after Him and look up to Him. When you allow Him a place in your life, He comes with a package that includes His joy and strength. This helps you to appreciate His abundant provisions. It helps you to accept your lot in this life.

> *From your lofty abode you water the mountains; the earth is satisfied with the fruit of your work. You cause the grass to grow for livestock and plants for man to cultivate, that he may bring forth food from the earth and wine to gladden the heart of man, oil to make his face shine and bread to strengthen man's heart.*
> **Psalm 104:13-15**

Joy Enables You to Cope with Life's Challenges

It is this same joy that enables you to work with all your might and enjoy the work you do. His joy enables you to work with all your strength even when you know your boss is not treating you right. It strengthens you to give your very best, knowing that it is God who truly rewards. It enables you to seek the good in your boss, knowing that God placed you there to be a blessing to His glorious name. The joy of the LORD enables you to love your spouse even when he or she does not relate well with you. It allows you the strength to do your portion of the bargain even when the other party fails to fulfill his or hers.

The joy of the Lord gives you hope in spite of the knowledge that physical death awaits you. Your hope is kept in the right perspective; your confidence is not in this life but in the hereafter. This same joy makes you unselfish because of the fact that you live not to please yourself but to please God. You work to make life better not for yourself *per se* but to create a better world for all mankind. You therefore work with all your strength to please God and serve others. In whatever you do, you need to know that no good deed done for others is ever wasted. Your life should have a positive impact on others.

> *"Let no one ever come to you without leaving better and happier."*
> **Mother Teresa**

This same joy, where it abounds, is associated with God's love, which surpasses all understanding. This joy helps you seek the welfare of others, too. It helps you to celebrate the victories of others and wish them happiness in all their endeavours. It enables you to feel the sorrow of others as you grieve when others grieve. It is not selfish joy. It is joy that does not see only self — it sees 'none-self', too.

> *"Those who are looking for happiness are the most likely not to find it, because those who are searching forget that the surest way to be happy is to seek happiness for others."*
> **Martin Luther King, Jr.**

The joy of the Lord causes you to see good in others and to give them the benefit of the doubt. It prevents you from being too critical of others. It keeps you always hopeful, causing you to persevere against all odds. It is this joy that keeps you in this world, in spite of all the negative things that may be happening around you. It helps you stand up on the inside against negative news. This joy is a prevailing joy.

Imprisoned but Still Joyful

The book of Philippians was written by the Apostle Paul while he was still under Roman house arrest. He was uncertain about his future; with all forms of doubts within and problems around him, he was able to maintain a good composure and an excellent attitude. He faced possible execution, yet he had inner peace. He was still thankful in spite of all he had gone through. He believed in God and was grateful for God's mercies. He still believed in a good God who was not only good to him but was also doing great things in the lives of others. Paul was a man who put the interest of others before his. His life on earth was lived to glorify God and to help others find and remain faithful to God (Philippians 1:25).

Paul was not just a humble servant of his master; he also encouraged others to emulate Christ's humility. He was of the opinion that complaining and arguing do not help you.

> *Do everything without complaining and arguing.*
> **Philippians 2:14**

Paul also directed the minds and hearts of his readers to pursue after God with all their hearts.

> *I want to know Christ and experience the mighty power that raised him from the dead. I want to suffer with him, sharing in his death, so that one way or another I will experience the resurrection from the dead.*
>
> **Philippians 4:10**

There is a power you get as you deeply pursue after God, and it causes every dying thing within you to come alive. Even joy can be resurrected by the power of God. Paul followed after God so deeply that he had inner strength to face the challenges he was going through. No wonder joy kept oozing out from within him and so many times — even under house arrest — he rather told the Philippi Christians to rejoice.

> *Rejoice in the Lord always; again I will say, rejoice. Let your reasonableness be known to everyone.*
>
> **Philippians 4:4-5**

The word 'reasonableness' stands for gentleness. It is found in souls that are broken and have surrendered to God's will and purpose. It is seen in lives that are given in to God and have understood that there is a higher purpose to this life beyond amassing wealth and material things, and competing amongst one another. It comes with an appreciation that life will not always go as you plan and that, many times, things go wrong. It accepts that even suffering has a place in what God wants to do in your life. People who appreciate this truth still wear smiles that radiate from the depths of their hearts, despite their troubles. They bring sunshine into the lives of others because they are almost always joyful.

> *"What sunshine is to flowers, smiles are to humanity. These are but trifles, to be sure: but scattered along life's pathway, the good they do is inconceivable."*
> **Joseph Addison**

Moulded by Suffering

Paul understood that suffering was part of the Christian journey. He understood that his very calling was tied to some form of pain and suffering for Christ's sake. For God to use you, He needs to refine and mould you. Paul understood that God had a plan for his life and that He rarely discloses the details of His plan. You need this understanding to keep your joy alive even as you go through difficult valleys in life. When you know what is going on, you remain confident that all will end well. However, when you are confused, perplexed, and confounded because of the challenges on every side, and you just do not understand what is happening, you tend to worry and stop hoping.

In God's plan for your life, there will be lonely days when it appears as though God has forsaken you. If you understand this truth, you will not let pain kill the inner joy in your heart. To get you into shape spiritually for what He has planned for you, God will allow you to go through some drills, to endure some blows and some fiery trials. All these will get you into the state where you can be a vessel God can use for noble purposes. This truth is so well articulated in J. Oswald Sanders book *Spiritual Leadership*, where he notes the following:

> *When God wants to drill a man*
> *And thrill a man*
> *And skill a man,*
> *When God wants to mould a man*
> *To plan the noblest part;*
> *When He yearns with all His heart*
> *To create so great and bold a man*
> *That all the world shall be amazed,*
> *Watch His methods, watch His ways!*
> *How He ruthlessly perfects*
> *Whom He royally elects!*
> *How He hammers him and hurts him,*
> *And with mighty blows converts him*
> *Into trial shapes of clay which only God understands;*
> *While his tortured heart is crying*
> *And he lifts beseeching hands!*
> *How he bends but never breaks*
> *When his good He undertakes;*
> *How He uses whom He chooses*
> *And with every purpose fuses him;*
> *By every act induces him*
> *To try His Splendour out —*
> *God Knows what He's about!*

Chapter 3
JOY UNDER FIRE

Chapter Three

> *Weeping may endure during the night and joy comes in the morning.*
> **Psalm 30:5**

Anything that seeks to kill your joy is attempting to paint God 'black'. Joy killers eventually and ultimately put a lot of doubt in your mind that there is a good God. Joy killers speak daily; they speak in several ways and at all times. Just as wisdom is always speaking, advising on your choices, so do the killers of joy. They scream at you from all directions, trying to keep you in pain and sorrow and at variance with God's will and purpose. There is a whirlwind of trouble blowing all over the face of the earth and in every nation and among every people of every culture. Weeping is a universal language, and so is laughter. Everybody experiences love, laughter, and mourning.

> *"Individual cultures and ideologies have their appropriate uses but none of them erase or replace the universal experiences, like love, weeping, and laughter, common to all human beings."*
> **Aberjhani,**
> *(Splendid Literarium, A Treasury of Stories, Aphorisms, Poems, and Essays)*

Everybody has a night season, when everything seems not to go well. Sometimes the pain you go through is not your fault. Yet, as much as you try, you cannot go through life without making mistakes. Often times these mistakes will come back to haunt you. As long as you remain on this side of the universe, you will be exposed to the biting winds of life's night seasons. Horrible things do happen that can shake the very core of your existence. It is very difficult to believe that God is good despite all the contrary physical evidence you are faced with. God has not left you to face the storms of this life alone. He promised you that so long as you remain close to Him and you listen and obey Him, He will be with you.

When you pass through the waters, I will be with you; and through the rivers, they shall not overwhelm you; when you walk through fire you shall not be burned, and the flame shall not consume you.
Isaiah 43:2

These promises do not immunize you against the storms of life. Whether you are a believer or not, trouble will knock on your door. The wind of evil often attempts to dull your ears to the voice and promise of God. God's voice is the voice of peace and tranquillity.

Chapter Three

When Trouble Strikes

> *"When we least expect it, life sets us a challenge to test our courage and willingness to change; at such a moment, there is no point in pretending that nothing has happened or in saying that we are not yet ready. The challenge will not wait. Life does not look back. A week is more than enough time for us to decide whether or not to accept our destiny."*
>
> **Paulo Coelho**
> *(The Devil and Miss Prym)*

The elements of nature many times become avenues through which you experience pain. Many times you are okay until trouble rears its ugly head to test your faith in the goodness of life and of the Creator who bequeathed it. Job was a man who feared God and kept away from all forms of evil. He was blessed to have children — and many of them, too. There were seven sons and three daughters who brought great joy to him. Job had a lot of material possessions — so much so that it made many envious. He had manservants and female servants.

Indeed, at that time, Job was amongst the *creme de la creme* of that society. He was the kind of 'perfect gentleman' who did everything he was supposed to do. He would not shirk his responsibilities and even went on to help others or met their expectations. Job was God fearing, prim, and proper, and to such people, it becomes very difficult for them to understand why things could go so wrong.

Many times, the reason why you do not face some forms of trouble, including natural disasters, is because you are shielded from them. There is a reason why you drive on the highway daily and you do not get involved in any accident. There is a reason why you may find yourself out on a stormy night and yet get to your doorstep safely, whilst others may not make it. There is a reason why you could navigate your vehicle through a flooded street whilst someone else was swept away.

> *"The longer I live, the more faith I have in Providence and the less faith in my interpretation of Providence."*
> **Jeremiah Day**

It is not your strength, your wisdom or anything of yours. It is because of divine providence. You are hedged from a lot of harm and you should be grateful and glad that every day you make it through the day unscathed.

Job was okay until so much trouble struck from outside. Whenever trouble strikes, you should learn to give God the benefit of the doubt. He is not the source of your pain, but, in His wisdom, He may have permitted it to get through for your ultimate good. His purpose will ultimately come through.

Struck from the Outside

You are tested daily as you make decisions that affect your own life and influence others directly or indirectly. You come to a crossroads on a daily basis as you make one decision or another. You always have to choose between one option and another. Whatever decision you make, it has consequences for the final outcome. Every time you are given options to choose from, never forget that you are being tested. Trouble also has a way of testing you. In the throes of pain and despair, your psyche, words, actions, and inactions will determine whether you will pass the test or not.

True joy is a bastion against the pressures you face from outside. It does not depend on external happenings, but, if the pressure from outside is sustained for long, your joy may be compromised as your thoughts, beliefs, actions, and inactions buffet you and open you to influences of doubt and sorrow, which lead, eventually, to deflation of joy. In the heat of pain, a spirit that is not robust can open up to external forces of doubt, fear, and, eventually, overwhelming sorrow. Overwhelming sorrow then drains your inner strength when the joy of the Lord ought to be your strength.

> *Then he said to them, "Go your way. Eat the fat and drink the sweet wine and send portions to anyone who has nothing ready, for this day is holy to our Lord. And do not be grieved, for the joy of the LORD is your strength."*
> **Nehemiah 8:10**

Your inner strength helps you to hold up against the storms of life. Joy is one of the bastions of your inner strength, and, when it is weak, you cannot face the vicissitudes of life's challenges. Strong people are joyful people, and joyful people are, indeed, strong souls. You need to have stable and solid emotions if you are going to go through this life and its challenges. I believe this may be the reason why God periodically allows some form of trouble to get through to you. In His wisdom, He is building up your inner strength, emotions, and psyche to handle different forms of external and internal pressures. As you learn how to stay strong in spite of all the darts, missiles, and the fires of this life, you will grow to be strong and dependable vessels of His glory.

When you pass through the waters, I will be with you; and through the rivers, they shall not overwhelm you; when you walk through fire you shall not be burned, and the flame shall not consume you.

Isaiah 43:2

Your ability to stay poised, calm, and emotionally strong in the storms of life is evidence of how strong you are. Weak people crumble at the least pressure. They cannot handle a series or chain of mishaps. You need to strengthen your spiritual and emotional muscles, too. It is for this reason that, often, trouble may be good for you. There is indeed a silver lining in every cloud. Face your challenges with courage and faith in a God who knows and understands what you do not know or understand. He sees beyond the present storm, and, if He permits it, then it is for a good reason.

> *If you faint in the day of adversity, your strength is small.*
> **Proverbs 24:10**

Are you going through undue stress, pain, frustration, disappointments, and all forms and shades of storms? You are not alone. Many see these problems daily. They marshal strength to handle their own problems as they learn to extend help and love to those who also go through their own peculiar challenges. Your own burden becomes bearable when you learn to lift the burdens of another person. As you unselfishly help others, make them happy, and relieve them of one burden or another, God's grace is released in abundance towards you to help deal with your own problems.

On your path to glory, you will be exposed to all forms of external pressures. Job was blessed in material and spiritual things. He had his family around him, and all was well with him. He had all forms of animals, which was a symbol of wealth in that period of time. When God considered him for the next level of promotion and elevation, God permitted the enemy to try Job. Tests and temptations do not come your way just to floor you. They are also used by God to take you to the next level of blessings. When the enemy throws weights of trouble at you, you can use these same weights as stepping stones to greater heights.

> *Now there was a day when his sons and daughters were eating and drinking wine in their oldest brother's house, and there came a messenger to Job and said, "The oxen were plowing and the donkeys feeding beside them, and the Sabeans fell upon them and took them and struck down the servants with the edge of the sword, and I alone have escaped to tell you." While he was yet speaking, there came another and said, "The fire of God fell from heaven and burned up the sheep and the servants and consumed them, and I alone have escaped to tell you." While he was yet speaking, there came another and said, "The Chaldeans formed three groups and made a raid on the camels and took them and struck down the servants with the edge of the sword, and I alone have escaped to tell you."*

Job 1:13-17

It is important that you do not allow the external things to gain so much value and influence over you. Material things may be affected, blighted, and even destroyed, yet you need to realize that, even though these are important, they should not be the most important things in your life. Your value systems need to change; your ideals, goals, and visions need to concentrate on building wealth and strength within your heart and not just within your external stores. The spirit is supposed to be of our utmost value and not material things. You cannot and will not carry any material thing with you when you expire, so learn to hold the material things of this life lightly.

The first hedge that gave way when Job was tested was the hedge covering the externals. That was what kept his beasts and other material possessions in place. When this hedge was removed, then disaster struck Job's oxen, donkeys, sheep, camels, and the servants who watched over them. Naturally, the servants acted as gatekeepers to this treasure, and, when the spiritual hedge was breached in the spiritual realm, these servants were wiped away, including all that they watched over.

The next hedge the enemy attacked was that which protected Job's sons and daughters.

> *While he was yet speaking, there came another and said, "Your sons and daughters were eating and drinking wine in the oldest brother's house, and behold, a great wind came across the wilderness and struck the four corners of the house, and it fell upon the young people, and they are dead, and I alone have escaped to tell you."*
> **Job 1: 18-19**

This hedge had been very strong and effective in spite of all the partying his sons got themselves involved in because their father sustained prayer on their behalf. This explains why you need to keep praying and making spiritual warfare on behalf of your children. When you do these, you ensure the hedge around them is intact and God's favor remains upon them.

> *His sons used to go and hold a feast in the house of each one on his day, and they would send and invite their sisters to eat and drink with them. And when the days of the feast had run their course, Job would send and consecrate them, and he would rise early in the morning and offer burnt offerings according to the number of them all. For Job said, "It may be that my children have sinned, and cursed God in their hearts." Thus Job did continually.*
>
> **Job 1:4-5**

You may invest material resources to keep your material possessions safe and protected, yet when it comes to your children, it is not enough. You need to protect them spiritually by sustained prayer, asking God to be merciful to them and to keep them safe.

You need to do what is in your power and ask for spiritual oversight and covering over your children. You may lose material investments and yet not be moved, however, when you lose your children, you would be callous to be unmoved. It is, therefore, not surprising that this blow was, indeed, devastating to Job.

> *Then Job arose and tore his robe and shaved his head and fell on the ground and worshiped. And he said, "Naked I came from my mother's womb, and naked shall I return. The LORD gave, and the LORD has taken away; blessed be the name of the LORD." In all this Job did not sin or charge God with wrong.*
>
> **Job 1:20-22**

Do not allow the devil and your illness to push you into thinking that God is out to get you. This is a big lie from the enemy to crush your life. Watch out against such crippling thoughts! Guard your thoughts, and, in your heart, sanctify Christ as your LORD. He cannot be against you! Get rid of this absurdly 'sick' thought!

> *"A sick thought can devour the body's flesh more than fever or consumption."*
> **Guy de Maupassant**

When disaster strikes, God expects you to think right and also manage your emotions well. You cannot handle your emotions well when you have wrong thoughts and thought processes. If you begin to believe that God is out to get you, it will set you on a downward spiral. Who can fight against God? Your entire soul, spirit, and body will collapse if you begin to believe that the omniscient Creator is against you.

Once you have the right thought processes, you can then mourn as a human being would — with feelings, because you are prone to pain and happiness. Yet, God does not expect you to be overwhelmed by the sorrow of your loss. Job was very sad and mourned his losses in sackcloth and ashes. In this harsh moment, Job did not stop doing what he had made a part and parcel of his life: He continued to worship God and maintained reverence, esteem, and honor for his Maker. He also did not lose sight of the fact that God was his Supplier and Divine Provider, and that he,

Job, added nothing to what God provided. God is the one who 'adds', and without His benevolence, you remain naked and not nurtured.

Job lived his life knowing that the material things and blessing of life can equally be removed in the same manner in which they can be added. Indeed, you have very little control over so many things and there is a limit to what you can do. Many of these misfortunes that grate you daily are also used to test your heart, your devotion, love, commitment, reverence, and dependence on God. In the darkest periods of your testing, you need to remember that God's name is still to be blessed.

Attacked in Person

One of man's greatest wealths is his health. You often do not appreciate good health until something bad happens. Good health enables you to enjoy the life God has graciously given unto you. Without health, you cannot enjoy the beautiful earth you have been bequeathed with upon which you make a living. The rising of the sun, the brightness of the day, the sunset, the coolness of a drizzle in the rainy season, the birds of the air, and the beauty of the ocean depths will all mean little when your health fails. Indeed, man has been known to offer all he has materially, emotionally, psychologically, and mentally in exchange for good health.

Good health comes with peace, and you need the peace of God to navigate through the turbulence of life. Men can attack your personality, they can lie about you, slander, or do all forms of evil against you, and you could choose not to be bothered. Yet all these unseen but hurtful forms of harm cannot be compared to the rage of devastating and incapacitating physical, mental, emotional, and psychological effects of lingering sickness.

The germ theory teaches that the root causes of disease are pathogens or germs. Scientifically this can be proven by empirical investigation; yet there have been several occasions when I have seen bizarre forms of sicknesses, with no scientific explanation as to what caused them. Many think such thinking is superstitious and should be discarded; yet there is another form of evidence from the Bible which reveals emphatically that there is a destroyer or ravager who works destruction and causes disease.

> *Behold, I have created the smith who blows the fire of coals and produces a weapon for its purpose. I have created the ravager to destroy,*
> **Isaiah 54:16**

Satan is the root cause of many diseases, and he has power to do so because of sin in your world.

> *Then Satan answered the LORD and said, "Skin for skin! All that a man has he will give for his life. But stretch out your hand and touch his bone and his flesh, and he will curse you to your face." And the LORD said to Satan, "Behold, he is in your hand; only spare his life." So Satan went out from the presence of the LORD and struck Job with loathsome sores from the sole of his foot to the crown of his head.*

Job 2:4-7

Lingering sickness can behave like a thief if permitted to do so, for the enemy of your soul can use it to steal many things from you. It can shift your attention from God and His love and divine provision to the gloom and despair of an uncertain outcome. When you shift your focus from God to the ravaging effects of disease, you break your link with the divine Provider and doubt, anger, and despair begin to fill your heart. These drive out God's presence, and, with it, your joy flies away.

You need to see God and His awesome greatness all around you. You need to see God's hand in the different shades, shapes, sizes, and fragrance of the flowers of the field. You need to see the Architect of Creation's strokes of genius in the patterns the clouds make in the sky. You have to focus on His dexterity in the creation of all the different kinds of beasts and their place on this earth. Focus is essential if you are to be able to deal with the trying times you meet here on this side of the universe.

Why Is Satan Messing with Me?

Satan will not mess with you if you do not matter. He has no time to waste on people going nowhere. Anyone who ever caught God's attention was doing something good. Anyone who caught Satan's attention was en route to a better place. The enemy has a knack for identifying great potential.

It is amazing that many do not even realize they are men and women of great destiny because they do not look successful. You thank God that sometimes trouble is sent your way by the enemy to jolt you into the reality that you are destined to be going places. Satan attacked Job because he was marked for glory. He was blessed, and God had the intention of putting more glory upon him.

> *There was a man in the land of Uz whose name was Job, and that man was blameless and upright, one who feared God and turned away from evil. There was born to him seven sons and three daughters. He possessed 7,000 sheep, 3,000 camels, 500 yoke of oxen, and 500 female donkeys, and many servants, so that this man was the greatest of all the people of the east.*
>
> **Job 1:1-3**

Satan brings trouble your way because he is jealous of what God is about to do with your life. When he smells glory from a distance, then he draws towards you. When he notices that God has great purpose for your life, he schemes to mess you up. He picks up signals of God's intended promotion for you, and then he begins to plan your destruction. He is in the background, trying to negotiate your downfall.

Thank God that Satan has not been given free rein over your life. Anytime God appears, He comes to bring you good news. When you see Satan in any place, he is there to spread evil. Satan has a purpose, too. He is used to push you to your next level of blessing. Do not allow the storm you are facing now to deflate your joy. As difficult as the situation may seem, God is still working some good in your life. As you pray for your healing or the healing of a loved one, also ask God to show you any other avenues opening up to sickness or disease. Sometimes there is something else happening oblivious to the normal eye. Just as Job did not understand where his illness came from, sometimes the root cause of an illness is unknown.

"When someone is in need of healing, it is good to pray for wisdom from our Father because there may be an open door to the sickness in their lives that they may not have considered."

Paul Silway
(Heaven I — Paradise: The City and Throne)

All things still work for the good of those who love God and are called according to his purpose. May God grant you wisdom to deal with your present challenge. Even your mistakes can work for your good if you place your life into the hands of God. Time is one of the greatest balms in life. It has a way of healing your gravest wounds and soothing your grieving soul. Take heart: God has not gone on a vacation! He is still on the throne in the highest heaven, and He will sit on the throne of your heart to reorder all the chaos in your life if you permit Him.

Chapter 4
WHEN NOTHING WORKS

God Is at Work

In your walk with God, there will be lonely days. There will surely be days of disappointment and days of sorrow. God never promised you a problem-free life. This earth is no comfort zone. The earth is troubled and inhabited by fallen beings who end up troubling themselves and everything around them. Serving God is no guarantee for a trouble-free and tranquil life. In fact, sometimes a life of storms is an indication that you may be walking right with God.

Trouble is often sent your way to throw you out of equilibrium and steal your joy. This occurs when you get angry and dissatisfied with God for what is happening around you or to you. The enemy is adept at getting you to believe that everything that goes wrong with you or around you is the doing of the Lord. The age-old question has often been, "How can a loving God allow trouble in your life?"

There will surely be seasons when nothing seems to be happening. You may have so many days when all seems stationary, and little or no progress is made. On the visible side of things, even the few things which were doing well may move into reverse gear. The few green shrubs may begin to wither, and there is very little activity. Life may seem to have come to a standstill, and, on the visible side, things may look like they are getting worse.

Like the season of winter, green life dries up, and many animals go into hibernation. This is the period in which animals reserve their energy, and their metabolism is in a very low mode. On the surface of the landscape, nothing seems to be changing, and everything looks and feels dry and even lifeless. However, at the cellular level, some things are still active, and there is life. This is the time some animals, like the wolf, grows its fur to ward off the cold and rain. Other animals, like the arctic fox, change their coat from a thin coat to a fluffy, thicker coat.

Time to Develop Your Spiritual Senses

When you enter into the winter seasons of your life, God is working to build spiritual strength within you. Unseen to your natural eyes, your resistance spiritually is undergoing ingenious adaptation and insulation against many forms of adversity. You need to change your perspective about the lean seasons of your life. As you go through this present dry season, you are going to come out stronger and hardier. Change keeps your senses keen and helps you adapt to your new environment.

"We are kept keen on the grindstone of pain and necessity."
H.G. Wells
(The Time Machine)

A major advantage animals who do well in the dry or winter seasons have is that they possess super senses. These senses give them an advantage during hunting of their prey. The grey owl, for example, has a keen sense of hearing and can detect subtle noise, even in the undergrowth. Those with sharp eyesight also win in the contest of survival of the fittest. During the dry or winter periods of your life, your senses have an opportunity to be sharpened. As you draw closer to God, He will help you develop a keen sense of spiritual hearing and vision. Knowing that there is an opportunity to draw closer to God and develop your spiritual senses should help you face these seasons with hope. Allow God to change you to adapt better to the difficulties around you. You will need the know-how to adapt to the changes that undo many people.

> *"The measure of intelligence is the ability to change."*
> **Albert Einstein**

No matter what happens to you or around you, God wants you to keep your joy. If you ask God, He will grant you the wisdom and intelligence to reign even in difficult terrain. You will surely not feel happy when things do not go well, but you will do well if you can still maintain some inner joy. There is no way you can get immunized against trouble, but God puts something in you to help fight every negative thing that will attempt to throw you into disequilibrium. This special gift is the joy He grants which helps you to adapt to change. It is not the joy of this world but the joy of the Lord.

Joy helps you to withstand bad news. It helps you to make the best of whatever situation you find yourself in. It cushions you against darts the enemy throws at your mind and spirit. It helps you to cope better with change. Inner joy helps the individuality within you to stand out when you need it most. All creatures are wired to stand against change. Your individuality will help to deal with and adapt differently to the changes you meet in life.

> *"Life is neither static nor unchanging. With no individuality, there can be no change, no adaptation and, in an inherently changing world, any species unable to adapt is doomed."*
>
> **Jean M. Auel**

The enemy uses dissatisfaction and disappointment in one way or another to push many to compromise and thereby forgo their covering in God. The enemy attempts to kill this joy by throwing all kinds of trouble at you. The joy of the Lord shields you from seeing how bad your situation truly is. Where God's joy abounds, this joy shields your eyes from seeing what you are not to see. You may be living in very trying circumstances, and yet God's love cushions you from the true effect of these circumstances. When nothing works, you would do well to concentrate on God and His love so you can maintain the joy of the Lord. When joy is in place, strength and wisdom to cope and master your new situation will abound to you.

Chapter Four

> *Though the fig tree should not blossom, nor fruit be on the vines, the produce of the olive fail and the fields yield no food, the flock be cut off from the fold and there be no herd in the stalls, yet I will rejoice in the LORD; I will take joy in the God of my salvation.*
> **Habakkuk 3:17-18.**

Where the joy of the Lord is absent, you get dissatisfied with yourself and with everybody around you. It is the joy of the Lord that sustains you in new and unfamiliar environments. When you always feel disadvantaged in life, this joy is absent. When you keep comparing yourself with others, this joy is absent. When you walk in envy and bitterness, this joy is absent. It is this joy that enabled John the Baptizer to rejoice when Jesus' ministry flourished whilst John's started dwindling. Situations around his life had changed overnight, and he had been able to adapt because he allowed God's joy to flow within him.

Where joy is present, envy is shut outside your heart. When heaven decides on a matter, men cannot do anything to change it. What has been permitted from above will prevail, no matter who objects. We need to learn not to fight what God does in the lives of people but try to be happy for them, knowing that our turn will surely come. If heaven determines that a man must increase, he will increase; if it is written that there must be a decrease, then human effort to kill this will not and cannot alter this.

> *"A person cannot receive even one thing unless it is given him from heaven…..He must increase, but I must decrease."*
>
> **John 3:27, 30**

When nothing seems to work, you must learn to concentrate on God and His love so you do not lose the joy of the Lord. It is the joy of the Lord that helps maintain your ground spiritually against the enemy's ploys to cause you to slip. Your spiritual estate is partly maintained by the joy of the Lord. Where the joy is absent, you will easily lose spiritual ground. Spiritual warfare becomes very difficult when things are not going well for you. You should ensure that you keep this joy when things are not going well, because you will be very ineffective in warfare should you lose it. When you lose the joy of the Lord, you equally lose your strength to the changes of life.

> *God, the Lord, is my strength; he makes me tread on my high places.*
>
> **Habakkuk 3:19**

Chapter 5
GOD IS NOT ASLEEP - LOOK FOR HIM

> *The eyes of the LORD are towards the righteous*
> *and his ears towards their cry.*
> **Psalm 34:15**

His Attention Is on You

It may not look like it, but God has His attention on you. One of the weaknesses as a human being is your inability to fully appreciate who you are: where you come from, what you possess or do not possess, where you could get to in this life independent of your experiences, how you presently view yourself, and how others view you. Your assessments, views, and perspectives are coloured by what you have been through, what others think and say about you and the stage upon which you stand to weigh your possibilities.

You are often oblivious of so many factors not exactly within your purview that directly — and, more importantly, indirectly — influence even how you feel about yourself on any given day. You are a frail creature who has been damaged by your fall into a sinful world which seeks to shape who you believe you are, your perception about who you are, your capabilities and shortcomings. You cannot see God, but He sees you all the time. You may not feel His presence, but you never exist outside His reach. He is everywhere; His presence transcends time and eternity. He is, He was, and He will always be. It is a fearful state to even believe that you can exist without the presence of God. Your weakness is to believe that you can make it outside of God. Your failure is indeed to start a journey in which God will not go with you, a marriage He is not a part of, and to step out on any life adventure unsure whether He has gone before you or not.

Men like Moses and Abraham, who walked with God, understood their total dependence on God. They knew that they would have lost any battle they had ventured into without God. They knew that stepping out of God's will spelt doom. It is better to live in a valley with God than to attempt to make it to the mountaintop without Him. How will you survive without Him?

> *"We shall steer safely through every storm, so long as our heart is right, our intention fervent, our courage steadfast, and our trust fixed on God."*
> **St. Francis De Sales**

Moses, the man of God, understood this truth. On their way to the Promised Land after their long years of servitude in Egypt, even whilst Israel was at Mount Sinai, Moses was hesitant to move a step further into a perceived blessing if God's presence was not going with them. There is no true blessing in this life without rest, and there can never be rest in any venture that God is very far from.

> *And he said, "My presence will go with you, and I will give you rest." And he said to him, "If your presence will not go with me, do not bring us up from here".*
> **Exodus 33:14**

Why Are You Looking Away?

Any success without God is doomed to fail. Any beginning without God is already an end. Any progress without God is retrogression. In your mind, you need to sanctify Christ as LORD and keep your thoughts saturated with His thoughts, His ways, His desires, and His commands. It is wrong to start the day without filling your thoughts with God. Think about His love, His care, His provision, His safety, His guidance, and His will. Desire to do His will, and His presence will keep you through your day.

> *"To fall in love with God is the greatest of all romances; to seek him, the greatest adventure, to find him, the greatest achievement."*
> **George Washington Carver**

God's presence is cultivated; it doesn't happen just by chance. If you learn to cultivate His presence by your thought inputs, patterns, desires, beliefs, and actions, you will not miss the presence of God when you need Him the most. God's attention is on you, and, for you to appreciate this, you also need to focus your attention on Him. You cannot see Him, but you have His written Word, His assurances through the psalms, songs, and hymns. If you are true to yourself, you will stretch out in faith and grasp His already-extended arm.

He has made the attempt long before you; He has always longed for your company, and He is already looking in your direction. Like the prodigal son who asked for his own share of the father's property, you also have demanded to live your life as you deem fit. Most often what you deem fit is away from God, His love and presence, His provision and care. The more you seek to live independent of God, the more you drive yourself away from His presence, love, and care.

As you demand your entitlements (from God) to live your life outside His will for you, you are directly negotiating a life of pain and sorrow. You will not realise it until it is too late; you will become lonely, frightful, and desolate. True loneliness is a life lived outside of God's presence and purpose. This explains why those who find success outside of God are always running a rat race of acquiring and pursuing many things they are never satisfied with. Satisfaction, peace, true success, and joy are a mirage in a journey away from God and His will and purpose for your life.

The things the world promises — fleeting joy, illicit sex, hard drugs, transient bliss, temporary wealth, fame that will not last, and other glamour — are all fading experiences. They can never truly satisfy since they are illusory. They can never fill the void within you that was created for an intimate relationship with your

Maker. Man, in his pursuit of all these without God, will sooner rather than later realise that it is a waste of time and effort.

Solomon came to a point after he tried it all, self-indulged in all forms of pleasure and said, 'It is all vanity after vanity'. After his several wives and concubines had driven his heart from God, he lived a self-indulgent life and came to conclude too late that he had wasted his life. When you follow your heart, your mind, and human wisdom instead of God, you will end where many end — futility. All your toil notwithstanding, without God, it is a waste.

> *I searched with my heart how to cheer my body with wine — my heart still guiding me with wisdom — and how to lay hold on folly, till I might see what was good for the children of man to do under heaven during the few days of their life. I made great works. I built houses and planted vineyards for myself. I made myself gardens and parks and planted in them all kinds of fruit trees. I made myself pools from which to water the forest of growing trees. I bought male and female slaves, and had slaves who were born in my house. I had also great possessions of herds and flocks, more than any who had been before me in Jerusalem. I also gathered for myself silver and gold and the treasure of Kings and provinces. I got singers, both men and women, and many concubines, the delight of the sons of man. So I became great and surpassed all who were before me in Jerusalem. Also my wisdom remained with me. And whatever my eyes desired I did not keep from them. I kept my heart from no pleasure, for my heart found pleasure in all my toil, and this was my reward for all my toil. Then I considered all that my hands had done and the toil I expended in doing it, and behold,*

> *all was vanity and a striving after the wind, and there was nothing to be gained under the sun.*
> **Ecclesiastes 2:3-11**

Depreciation by Dissociation

Everything of value God blesses you with begins to lose its true value when you move away from Him. God is the constant; every other thing is a negative variable that will negate your life. A journey away from God is a journey towards progressive setback. A mind-set that fights the existence of God is a mind-set that is going down and down into abysmal depths of no lasting value.

Prodigality is anti-God, and any anti-God person begins to waste his life. In the natural state, you will think and believe that you are really enjoying life, but it is a lie. In your proclivity, you are unaware that you are trading away some very precious things you may never retrieve or recover again.

It is a fact that many 'illicit' practices have spiritual implications, some of which will scar you for life and rob you of a glory that cannot be replaced. Physical acts that directly or indirectly break the moral codes of God are often tied to open ways into the depths of your spirit, leaving you vulnerable to spiritual ambush by evil forces. Some treasures that are squandered by reckless living are not replaceable.

Chapter Five

> *Not many days later, the younger son gathered all he had and took a journey into a far country, and there he squandered his property in reckless living.*
> **Luke 15:13**

Immediately, you leave God, and you begin to walk in darkness and on a road to a futile destination. You open your life up for bandits to attack, and they will rob you of your talents, value, and worth. This explains why many who move away from God soon begin to live lives of low self-worth. They claim a life of independence, but the truth is that they have become slaves to their passions and desires. Sooner or later, they begin to exchange their glory for shame by indulging in all manner of inhuman and ungodly acts that degrade the human soul and bring men to levels even lower than beasts.

When you wander away from God, the enemy has a field day! He will tear you apart and will finally possess your soul. Your appetite will change for the worse, and soon you will desire, indulge in, and find fulfilment in strange activities. Soon you will be hooked on the unnatural; you will do everything in your power to satisfy your ungodly desires.

> *And he was longing to be fed with the pods that the pigs ate, and no one gave him anything.*
> **Luke 15:16**

These desires make you unclean and allow for more demonisation. Demonic control can be very subtle. You will not even know you have been demonised. These spirits operate under cover and manipulate men to do their whims and caprices. Like puppets in the hands of puppeteers, your life is no longer 'independent' but subjugated to the control of unseen forces. This explains why breaking these appetites become a struggle.

He Came to Himself

There are people who are always moody, and they believe it is normal. Others are always sad, and they also feel that it is a normal experience. Some, too, are always pessimistic; they see nothing good in anything or anybody. These are not normal at all and may be the external evidence of evil controlling influences. It is possible that you are being manipulated by evil influences without you knowing it.

There are more people under subtle demonic influence than those who are under obvious influence. When you are under an external influence, you do things you are not supposed to do, say things you would not say on your own, and act inappropriately. Your appetite is altered to suit the appetites and desires of these unseen but very active negative forces.

> *But when he came to himself, he said, 'How many of my father's hired servants have more than enough bread, but I perish here in hunger!'*
> **Luke 15:17**

Reach Out to God

Any time you realise there is a breach in the relationship you have with God, most likely, *you* have moved and not God. God's love is abounding. He normally has His hands stretched out to draw you back to Himself when you start to wander away. So many activities call for your attention. For many, before they even realise it, God has been thrown behind as being of less priority.

All this, too, is the plan of the enemy. Other issues meander their way into your busy life and into your already-crowded schedule, hence, you have very little time for a solid relationship with God. Soon, even though God calls, alerts, and even screams to get your attention, you do not hear Him. When you fail to keep intimacy with God, your spirit becomes weak, and a weak spirit fails to relate well with God.

> *Because I have called and you refused to listen, have stretched out my hand and no one has heeded, because you have ignored all my counsel and would have none of my reproof, I also will laugh at your calamity; I will mock when terror strikes you like a storm and your calamity comes like a whirlwind, when distress and anguish come upon you.*
>
> **Proverbs 1:24-27**

You need to go back and mend your relationship with God. What has taken over your life? Why do you not have time for God and His word? Have you ignored God for so long that you cannot hear Him speak to you anymore? Are you walking in blatant disobedience to His word and possibly missed His direction for your life? When is the last time you genuinely called out to Him? If there are things you need to forsake, do so now, for tomorrow may be too late. If you genuinely ask God to forgive you for ignoring Him for all this while, He will pardon you.

> *"One of the most arduous spiritual tasks is that of giving up control and allowing the Spirit of God to lead our lives."*
>
> **Henri Nouwen**

You cannot live your life on your terms and still expect God to lead you. You will need to gather courage and say no to some things that fight God's glory so that He will restore your life. Wickedness is not just murder or any other out rightly abominable acts. Forsaking your first love for God is also seen as wickedness. Not finding time for God is wickedness against your own soul, for being absent from God is spiritual death — a state in which your spirit and soul eventually translate into the natural physical realm as retrogression, suffering, lack, and a life of no peace.

> *Let the wicked forsake his way; and the unrighteous man his thoughts; let him return to the LORD, that he may have compassion on him, and to our God, for he will abundantly pardon. For my thoughts are not your thoughts, neither are your ways my ways, declares the LORD.*
> **Isaiah 55:7-8**

It is time to return back to the LORD. Gather not only in word but also a heart bent on genuinely seeking after God, and He will hear you. He will open His doors to you that will change the state of your soul and bring peace into your life. Your life is about to change for good as you give God his rightful place.

Chapter 6
DO NOT THROW HOPE OUT

Overburdened with Desolation?

> *Oft in danger, oft in woe,*
> *onward, Christians, onward go;*
> *bear the toil, maintain the strife,*
> *strengthened with the bread of life.*
>
> *Onward, Christians, onward go,*
> *join the war, and face the foe;*
> *will ye flee in danger's hour?*
> *Know ye not your Captain's power?*
>
> *Let not sorrow dim your eye;*
> *soon shall every tear be dry:*
> *let not fears your course impede;*
> *great your strength, if great your need.*
>
> *Let your drooping hearts be glad;*
> *march in heavenly armour clad;*
> *fight, nor think the battle long:*
> *soon shall victory wake your song.*
>
> *Onward then in battle move;*
> *more than conquerors ye shall prove:*
> *though opposed by many a foe,*
> *Christian soldiers, onward go.*
>
> **White, Henry Kirke**

The night of pain and sorrow often seems to drag on and on. Your sleep brings you no rest, and your mind is plagued with distressing thoughts of doom and sadness. You toss and turn on your bed night after night because sleep is stolen from you, and you cannot see the end of all this trouble. Your heart is troubled, and fear trails your very steps. You are frightened even by your own shadow. Where shall your hope come from when all your days run so swiftly, with no change in sight to this miserable life? You hide under the cover of loneliness and keep yourself far away from all who have been your acquaintances. You dare not let them see what has become of you.

Your heart has become heavy with the burden of your unending woes. Your eyes refuse to see any good, and the grave lingers on your mind. In the anguish of your spirit, you spew out bitterness. You are even unaware of the depth of how poisonous you have become and how low your soul has sunk. When you have no hope, your labour becomes more burdensome. Even little things become like a chore. Hopelessness makes your days long and dreary. It stops the clock of progress. Hopelessness is a thief of the present, and this includes all the opportunities it carries. Do not allow the mess of the past to rob you of today's opportunities.

"Yesterday is history, tomorrow is a mystery, today is a gift of God, which is why we call it the present."
Bil Keane

Hopelessness kills your appetite, sweeps away your joy, and blinds your eyes to all the good things in your life. It convinces its victims that they are totally messed up and their years have been wasted.

It dresses its victims with sackcloth and serves them with the gall of bitterness. It robs people of their sleep, giving them long and lonely nights with no opportunity for a better tomorrow. Do not entertain it!

Job fell into this state. Hopelessness paid him a visit, and his speech and life were negatively influenced. With a body ravaged by disease and infirmity, the visitor sent worms into his flesh and afflicted him with physical and spiritual torment. His speech was understandably full of sadness.

> *"Has not man a hard service on earth, and are not his days like the days of a hired hand? Like a slave who longs for the shadow, and like a hired hand who looks for his wages, so I allotted months of emptiness, and nights of misery are apportioned to me. When I lie down I say, 'When shall I arise?' But the night is long, and I am full of tossing till dawn. My flesh is clothed with worms and dirt; my skin hardens, then breaks out afresh. My days are swifter than a weaver's shuttle and come to their end without hope".*
>
> **Job 7:1-6**

Trouble on Every Side

In the state of hopelessness, you gradually become convinced that everything has set itself against you. The elements of nature seem to have been commanded to join the army that assails your soul. Who do you blame for all this? If the Almighty controls all things, then it must be God, so your burdened heart convinces you. Your conscience searches from within: which of your many sins are you being punished for? He must be too callous as not to forgive your sin. In the darkness of your soul's pain, you ponder over your past by trying to pinpoint the sins and mistakes you have made that may have opened the doors of misfortune into your life. The favour and blessing of God seem to have left you. The enemy makes you believe that God is bent on keeping you under bondage, pain, and torment.

How long will you not look away from me, nor leave me alone till I swallow my spit? If I sin, what do I do to you, you watcher of mankind? Why have you made me your mark? Why have I become a burden to you? Why do you not pardon my transgression and take away my iniquity? For now I shall lie in the earth; you will seek me, but I shall not be."

Job 7:19-21

It takes grace to still believe in God when you are in the dungeon of hopelessness. There are not many who will still look up to the Maker when all hope is lost. You have been made to believe that God has long left you. The enemy of your soul will attempt to make you believe that God is behind all the pain you are going through. Choose to still trust and lean on God. Like Job, confess to the enemy that, though God appears to slay you, you will still hope in Him. He may have permitted the current storm for a reason, and He is always right.

> *Though he slay me, I will hope in him...*
> **Job 13:15**

Move towards the Light

There are dark moments in every life, but you need to always move towards the light. How difficult it is, when you are in the thickness of the storm, to believe that the Lord is still your Fortress and Deliverer. If He was truly your Rock and your Salvation, how did He allow this to get to you? When you call upon the Lord, you believe that He will save you from all your troubles, yet storms hit you daily, and misfortunes do not exempt the believer in God. Indeed, there are countless situations where God permitted the cords of death to surround His Own. You may presently be encompassed with torrents of destruction, and the snares of death may be starring at you.

In your distress, do not throw in the towel. Rather, call upon God. Cry out to Him, for your cry will surely get to His ears. The earth upon which you stand may be reeling, and the foundations of your hope, faith, and truth may presently be trembling. There may be thunder all around you, and your enemies may be too many and too strong for you to handle. You still need to get to the place of hope and faith, where you are assured that there is a good God who still delights in you and will help you.

You may have kept to the ways of God and lived a good life, yet trouble and doom have visited you. You may have followed all God's ways, His rules, and statutes, yet darkness has met you in broad daylight. It will help you to remember that bad things also happen to good people. The merciful do not always receive mercy, and the loving do not always receive goodwill. All the troubles you have gone through or will ever face will sharpen your vision and broaden your outlook on life. You will 'see' better because of the darkness you have endured. Trouble will help you appreciate all the blessings in your life which you have taken for granted.

"I like the night. Without the dark, we'd never see the stars."
Stephenie Meyer
(Twilight)

Evil souls may have sent their rubbish to your address. Greedy people may have forsaken you in the wilderness of life. They may have snatched light from your path, leaving you in utter darkness, with little hope for a good future. As you walk through this darkness, know that God is the One who will light your lamp. He will lighten your darkness and refresh your torn soul. May you leap over every wall of setback, and may grace find you to help you run through every troop of opposition. Still choose to take refuge in God, for He is the shield for all those who take refuge in Him.

There is no Rock like Jehovah. He will equip you with strength in this period of pain. Do not lose hope, for hopelessness will deprive you of God's help. Your feet can be strengthened again, like that of the deer. With hope, you will be set secure upon the heights of the land. God's right hand will find all who choose to hope against all hope. Indeed, do not fret, for God's gentleness will reach you and make you great. You may be down, but you are definitely not out. You cannot afford to give up, for hope will grant you the strength for the battle ahead. With hope, your enemies will turn and flee from you.

Do not let any situation make you believe that you are already dead. Remember that the dead cannot cry out for help, but the living do. A live dog is better than a dead lion, so choose to live, and do not lose hope. Many people may be against you now, but hope in God will deliver you eventually from the strife of men. Hope will exalt you above those who rise up against you and rescue you from violent men. Hope, indeed, will lead you into God's steadfast love and ultimately open a door of escape into His salvation. Embrace hope even in the storm, and you will be embracing life.

> *For who is God, but the LORD? And who is a rock except our God? — the God who equipped me with strength and made my way blameless. He made my feet like the feet of a deer and set me secure on the heights. He trains my hands for war, so that my arms can bend a bow of bronze. You have given me the shield of your salvation, and your right hand supported me, and your gentleness made me great. You gave a wide place for my steps under me, and my feet did not slip.*
>
> **Psalm 18:31-36**

The Benefits of Hope

> *"Hope is the thing with feathers*
> *That perches in the soul*
> *And sings the tune without the words*
> *And never stops at all."*
>
> **Emily Dickinson**

With hope as a shield, you will know that your Redeemer lives, and you will, indeed, see His salvation. You will not be reduced to skin and bones, and your dear life will not be snuffed out. Your enemies will shut their mouths, and those who sneered at you will stop. The vigour of your youth will be restored, and you will rise from the ground and shake off the ashes. You will be delivered from the venom of the viper and the poison of the cobra.

With hope by your side, you will escape the bronze arrow and the iron spear. Doom will fly away like a dream, and your testimony will be engraved in a rock. Your heart will not faint but will rejoice in the deliverance of God. Those who looked at you and were appalled will look at you and rejoice. As you hold onto the rope of hope, your lamp will not be put out. May your soul find God's peace, and may destruction be far from you with hope by your side. Inner truth, when it is there and acknowledged, will grant you strength to look beyond your present pain. May your portion be one of hope and life. Surely, your redeemer lives, and at last He will show up for your redemption.

Chapter Six

> *For I know that my Redeemer lives, and at last he will stand upon the earth.*
> **Job 19:25-26**

Chapter 7
ESSENTIAL REMEMBRANCE

Your Thoughts Will either Arm You or Disable You

> *"Well, if it can be thought, it can be done, a problem can be overcome,"*
>
> **E.A. Bucchianeri**
> *(Brushstrokes of a Gadfly)*

The power of memory is a great gift God gave to man. It is a gift the enemy also exploits to your disadvantage, but it can be used to sustain your God-given joy. So many times you are prone to remember negative things whilst you so easily forget the good things in your life. You remember every single bad thing others have done and do not remember the several good things these same people have done for you. This is a great wrong, and you need grace to overlook the mistakes of those dear to you and to remember all the good and love they have shown you. Remember that your thoughts will either arm you or disable you.

Your fallen nature appreciates the negative more than it does the positive. This is a great weakness which the enemy likes to play upon in order to get you distraught emotionally. Remembrance of the good things others have done is far better than remembrance of the negative. Remembrance that augurs well for your well-being and happiness is what I term 'essential remembrance'. Essential remembrance is critical to your health and sense of well-being.

One of the reasons God gave you this type of remembrance was because you need it direly to discomfit the works of the enemy. A key tool used by evil forces entrusted with the task of keeping men depressed is negative remembrance. These depressive influences are rendered impotent by positive thoughts that result from remembering the good things God and others have done for you. The dynamics and *modus operandi* of God is beyond human comprehension. Many times God allows the 'enemy' to make you feel that he is in control and that God does not care.

You may go through one form of trouble after another. Hardly do you move from one valley before you get messed up in another. The enemy, being who he is, will keep reminding you about all the troubles you have been through and seen. God's way of breaking these negative thought patterns is often not by commanding these forces to leave you or by prayer alone. Prayer works wonders against negative thought patterns. Sometimes the negative thoughts come in a sequential manner, and they seek to flood your soul with helplessness. These may be spiritual fiery darts shot into your thoughts to keep you mentally frustrated and depressed.

In fact, I have realised that, with some people, prayer alone does not draw them out of the 'clouds of depression.' For these people, persistent listening to God's word and words of hope are often followed by gradual change. When they begin to see some good come their way, they begin to glow gradually like a dim lamp. This explains why you could be emotionally low for a long time, with virtually no help until something dramatic turns things around.

The trend of bad memories is broken when you begin to perceive good thoughts in your mind. You do not need to hear only good news, but you need to begin to see great things happening in your life.

> *"Remember not the former things, nor consider the things of old. Behold, I am doing a new thing; now it springs forth, do you not perceive it? (Emphasis mine).*
> **Isaiah 43:18-19**

When we begin to envisage good coming our way after a long drought, it comes with power to break the back of negative thoughts. God then reminds us of where we have been before and how far He has brought us. Essential remembrance is made more vocal and vivid in the setting of past misfortune. This helps us keep our joy in the setting of any other misfortune that will attempt to raise its head.

Your Current Challenges Are Working for Your Good

God allows you to go through difficult times and then brings you into His season of restoration and blessing so you can learn how to maintain and hold onto the joy of the Lord. Those who have not gone through much in life cannot appreciate when good comes, and, therefore, they are unable to sustain God's enduring joy. Whenever trouble knocks on your door, remember that the good Lord may have permitted it to prepare you for His mega-plan for you in the future. He is working everything for your good. Your current challenges will prepare you for tomorrow's breakthroughs.

"If we are not allowed to deal with small problems, we will be destroyed by slightly larger ones. When we come to understand this, we live our lives not avoiding problems, but welcoming them as challenges that will strengthen us so that we can be victorious in the future."

Jim Stovall
(The Ultimate Gift)

Remember always that it takes essential remembrance to break negative thought patterns and that essential remembrance works best when you have been in the 'valley' before. May essential remembrance arm you with strength to keep your joy no matter how bad your situation may be. Whenever the enemy tries to put you down in the day of misfortune, may you have the grace to focus your mind or thoughts on good things. The ability to focus on the positive does not come easily. It comes only with effort and practice. This is a major reason why you need to keep God's words of encouragement and hope in the arena of your mind. This you must try to do to ensure that depressive and fearful thoughts do not keep you bound.

Chapter Seven

> *For God gave us a spirit not to fear but of power and love and self-control.*
> **2 Timothy 1:7**

> *For God hath not given us the spirit of fear; but of power, and of love, and of a sound mind.*
> **2 Timothy 1:7- KJV**

You have the power to focus on the positive. You have the power to push away negative thoughts. The spirit behind fear and depression is a spirit of slavery that draws its captives back into cycles of fear. Satan is a hard taskmaster who rejoices in seeing his captives bound and chained to fear, offering his victims no liberty. God loves you, and if you open up to Him and His word, He will flood your soul with His love and peace. The more of His love you receive and embrace, the less fear will control your life. Indeed, perfect love casts out fear.

> *There is no fear in love, but perfect love casts out fear. For fear has to do with punishment, and whoever fears has not been perfected in love.*
> **1 John 4:18**

Chapter 8
WHEN FRIENDS FAIL US

Know Your Friends

> *"Suffering has been stronger than all other teaching, and has taught me to understand what my heart used to be. I have been bent and broken, but — I hope — into a better shape."*
> **Charles Dickens**
> *(Great Expectations)*

It is a fact that your friends will fail you. They may not be there when you need them the most. Many of those who wound you will be those close to you. Friends are expected to be loyal and friendly with all the good and nice stuff, but the truth is that they are human, and they will fail and disappoint you.

It is a reality and, indeed, not surprising, to know that all cords of friendships or relationships have different levels of ties that may give way under different levels of external or internal forces. This implies that these cords are all subject to failure. Even amongst professing and practicing Christians, there are scores of stories of betrayals, and, many times. these may be lethal. Of course, when a believer betrays you, you feel let down and, to some extent, even by the God they profess to represent.

Indeed, he who seeks to have friends must first be friendly. When you attach God to yourself and let all and sundry know that you are godly, then, obviously, more is expected of you.

He who withholds kindness from a friend forsakes the fear of the Almighty. My brothers are treacherous as a torrent-bed, as torrential streams that pass away...

Job 6:14-16

Friends with Benefits

A lot of people in your life who have the tag of 'friends' hanging around their necks are really in the friendship for the benefits they get from it. Your selfish human nature is glued so tightly to your being that it will take eternity to get it out of you. Even when you are indeed saved, redeemed, and cleansed by the blood of Jesus, you still have to allow Christ to help you deal with fleshly drives, including selfishness. Your selfish self and your selfish friends all expect something from others, and, when that does not come, you not only feel disappointed, but you quickly, perhaps subtly, try to disengage yourself from them.

You become emotionally detached, mentally distanced, and removed psychologically from others. Your so-called 'friends' were all in your life to receive, receive, and receive. They may be walking around and smiling with you, but they are carrying empty trunks to load goodies and whisk them away. They are like caravans in the desert of life — coming a long, long way with great expectations that you will heavily provide for them, their needs, their wants, and maybe even the needs and wants of their friends and families. They are indeed hoping and looking for benefits out of this association, even though they make you believe that they do not really need anything from you.

> *The caravans turn aside from their course; they go up into the waste and perish. The caravans of Tema look, the travelers of Sheba hope. They are ashamed because they were confident; they come there and are disappointed.*
>
> **Job 6:18-20**

When your light goes out suddenly, they do not need you anymore. They now see you as a burden, a bother, and a weight they cannot afford to carry along. You have now become a liability to them. They prefer not to know you. They weigh what you can now offer them, and they no longer think you are of any more value to them. Truly the rich have many friends, and the poor — oh, what a pity — they have nothing of worldly value to offer. The selfish now see little value in you, so why should they still stick with you? To them, you have become the scum of the earth — you are of no value to them, and they will throw you away. How you have now become so much of a bother that all your selfish friends are running away from you?

> *For you have now become nothing; you see my calamity and are afraid.*
>
> **Job 6:21**

They have gotten closer and seen your grave weaknesses, your frailties, your incompetency, your lack, or your poverty and they feel disappointed. Hence, they do what they think is normal — desert you. The viciousness and cunning of selfish mankind is immense. When they see that you have little they can benefit from, they take away the camouflage and wash off all the mascara, including their feigned pleasantness, to expose their dark and wicked hearts. In this state, they can do the unthinkable, say the unspeakable, and proclaim without shame how useless you have become. They will voice their doubts and overlay even their doubts with shades of gray, not black-and-white.

What can the selfish and the disappointed not do? Nothing is beyond them, therefore, do not be surprised that they deserted you in the wilderness for wild beasts to devour. They had no inner mercy all along — they were clad in holy attire just to make an impression.

> *You would even cast lots over the fatherless,*
> *and bargain over your friend.*
> **Job 6:27**

Indeed, they have associated with you all this while and were wolves in sheep's clothing.

They Act as Gods!

One of the surprises I have met in life is a person who called himself or herself a friend and even better than that — 'family' — and who, all of a sudden assumes the status of a god when misfortune strikes you. These people speak like they know it all and have experienced it all! What is even sadder is that some of these are your peers, your contemporaries, people of your own generation. Some of them are not even fathers or mothers, but still, they assume a 'paternalistic' attitude toward you, even though they have no right to exercise that form of control over a wounded person. Suddenly, because of your challenge, they assume 'terrestrial and celestial' authority status to dissect your condition and tell you why you are no good.

They assume the position as God's lawyers, sent to put you in your place. They explain to you why you deserve no mercy. They claim you have forgotten God and have lost touch with all His blessing. Instead of sitting with the wounded to share in their grief, they often come with all forms of theology to lecture you. It is as if you are a junior student, taking lessons on repentance.

> *"Can papyrus grow where there is no marsh? Can reeds flourish where there is no water? While yet in flower and not cut down, they wither before any other plant. Such are the paths of all who forget God; the hope of the godless shall perish. His confidence is severed, and his trust is a spider's web. He learns against his house, but it does not stand; he lays hold of it, but it does not endure. He is a lush plant before the sun, and his shoots spread over his garden. His roots entwine the stone heap; he looks upon a house of stones. If he is destroyed from his place, then it will deny him, saying, 'I have never seen you.' Behold, this is the joy of his way, and out of the soil others will spring. Behold, God will not reject a blameless man, nor take the hand of evildoers".*

Job 8:11-20

These and many other words were said by Job's ignorant, self-believing friends who tried to explain why misfortune had visited him. Their theology of pain and suffering was flawed, and you can expect the same when you meet misfortune. There are things man can never explain. Some things are hidden, and it is folly for mankind to believe they can fully understand or interpret God's ways with man. When a man's ways please the LORD, sometimes God allows some things he does not and cannot understand to come his way for His own good purpose. You should never misinterpret current situations as rejection from God. Some 'chastisements' that come your way are permitted because you are special to God, and He may be using them for His own great purpose. If you do not believe me, read — and heed — the book of Job!

Men Will Celebrate Your Fall

Do not believe all who greet you in the morning, for people are not who they claim to be. In the evening, you should not be surprised if these people return your greeting with insult. Though it is not healthy to walk around suspecting everybody, those who bow before you in respect today will turn their back on you when your predicament changes.

Many who cried "crown Him, crown Him" were the same people who later changed the tune of their song to "crucify him, crucify him." Indeed, we should not glory in the acclaims of men but tread cautiously in this life. When listening to a song, follow the words and the tune carefully, for soon the tune may change and the words might be reversed. It is simply wisdom not to put too much confidence in mere mortals.

Not many who walk with you as peers today will continue to share from their calabash with you tomorrow when misfortune knocks. It is a fact that, sooner rather than later, in the midst of life's vicissitudes, men metamorphose into something you will not like. They will magnify themselves over and against you. Do not be flattered by even close relations, for men change just as the leaves of a tree dry up.

When trouble visits your abode, people may behave like they do not know you; some will treat you as if you are a stranger. You may call, and even your own children may pretend not to hear. Your husband or wife may now see you as a great burden. When misfortune knocks on your door, evil sees it as an opportunity to enter in along with it. Friends and acquaintances along your paths can — and will — take advantage of. Is it surprising to discover that there is a domino effect with misfortune? These can be moments when evil is stirred up and cascades all around you. When misfortune comes, your 'friends' and relatives can fly away like birds that have seen a hunter close by.

> *The guests in my house and my maidservants count me as a stranger; I have become a foreigner in their eyes. I call to my servant, but he gives me no answer; I must plead with him with my mouth for mercy. My breath is strange to my wife, and I am a stench to my children of my own mother. Even young children despise me; when I rise they talk against me. All my intimate friends abhor me, and those whom I loved have turned against me*
>
> **Job 19:15-19**

Every misfortune is but a passing visit. We need to learn not to make decisions and judge people by their sudden misfortune. Yet as human and evil as men are, they make decisions and act as if they know it all. People do not align to friends or relations; many align to whatever situation will benefit them. May your alliances be born out of a true heart and not out of a situation. Over the years, you do not lose friends — your situation helps you to keep the true ones and discard the opportunists.

Nothing Good Will Come out of Our Lives — So They Say

Those who dislike you assess your situation and conclude that God is finished with you, and, therefore, they condemn you to a life of misery. Proud people will see only doom in your unfortunate situation. In their hearts, you are down and out. They may not say it out loud, but, when they look at you, all they see is that you are down and out. In their silent thoughts, they believe they have seen your end. They imagine the very worst for you: all they see in your life now and in the future is pain, dread, destruction, anguish, poverty, darkness, emptiness, unfruitfulness, bareness, and all forms of trouble.

They are mistaken, for most of the time, God has not finished with you yet. Like Job, weeping may endure for the night, but joy comes in the morning. Expect it! You have been through hellfire and a very difficult place. God is about to reverse the trend. Get ready for the day of fresh beginnings. God has just started with you. You will soon forget the problems of yesterday. Believe it, and you will receive it! Refuse to mourn anymore. Excessive mourning can act as a curse. Drop it! Brighten your eyes; joy and restoration are just around the corner. Refuse to see all people as unfaithful. You need to still trust somebody, for, without trust, your life will become miserable.

"Everyone suffers at least one bad betrayal in their lifetime. It's what unites us. The trick is not to let it destroy your trust in others when that happens. Don't let them take that from you."
Sherrilyn Kenyon
(Invincible)

Chapter 9
EXCESSIVE MOURNING

Liberation from Excessive Sorrow

> *"Some grief shows much of love,*
> *But much of grief shows still some want of wit."*
> **William Shakespeare**
> *(Romeo and Juliet)*

Life is lived in stages. It has been said that 'life is lived forwards but understood backwards'. It is a fact, though, that, many times, God allows you to go through experiences you do not and may not understand all the days of your life. Life's cycle is full of incidents, and, whether you are prepared for them or not, they will happen. There will be some losses, some failures, and some disappointments. You will lose some friends and loved ones, but you need courage to close these chapters after you have mourned the loss and continue living to write the remaining chapters of your own life with hope and bravery.

Some disappointments will also be sent to your mail, many from people who are supposed to be close to you. When you go through disappointments, you should learn to move on. God expects you to move on! But how can you move on when you get trapped in a state of prolonged mourning? One of the enemy's chief strategies against your advancement is to saddle you with disappointment, sorrow, and despair.

The enabling God graces you with to do many exploits is crippled by a spirit of despair and mourning. Despair and mourning are truly a garb of heaviness the enemy cunningly puts upon people to immobilize them at least for a while. It is a pity how men get stuck to a place in life and are manipulated in their emotions by the enemy to keep them fixated on their past sad experiences.

There is a place for mourning in the life of every person, but mourning, when not handled well, draws you into a state of spiritual stupor where mighty men and women are immobilized though they are endowed with great power. All who just weep and lament and continue in it for long hardly ever make any progress.

"When you weep and lament, you will struggle to achieve and rejoice."
Auliq Ice

Some stories that do not have a happy ending need to be closed and the documents shelved and kept under lock and key. It is amazing how your memory is quick to remember things you are not supposed to remember. Sin has conditioned you to gravitate towards what has hurt you, keeping you in a state of disappointment and grief. Your mind is quick to remember negative things that keep you feeling sorry for yourself and others. When misfortune hits, the unseen enemy gets excited because he has another opportunity to slow down your spiritual and physical progress by bringing misfortune to your thoughts.

Disappointments, despair, and excessive mourning have the power to cause you not to see the new things God is about to do in your life. Often, you are blinded to the next move of God when you remain in mourning. This is a crafty manipulation of the enemy to keep you stuck in life. It is, therefore, not surprising that God often sends others to shake you out of your spiritual stupor.

> *Arise and shine, for your light has come, and the glory of the LORD has risen upon you. For behold, darkness shall cover the earth, and thick darkness the peoples; but the glory will be seen upon you. And nations shall come to your light, and kings to the brightness of your rising.*
> **Isaiah 60:1-3**

God moves often to bless you beyond your wildest dreams, especially after major disappointments, hence, you should not allow the enemy to keep you trapped in your disappointment.

> *Instead of your shame there shall be a double portion; instead of dishonor they shall rejoice in their lot; therefore in their land they shall possess a double portion; they shall have everlasting joy.*
> **Isaiah 61:7**

Prolonged Mourning Is a Spirit

In the African setting, it is easy to identify a person in mourning just by the cloth they put on. We Africans put on black clothing to signify the loss of a loved one. This enables even those who are remote, in terms of position, to make them out easily. Funerals have become a part of the African culture. You celebrate death so much that funeral grounds eventually become fun fairs. You, in your state of mourning, are drawn to others who are also mourning, just by the cloth or dress you put on. God does not expect you to stay in a state of mourning for long. He expects you to move on!

Prolonged mourning is the work of enemy spirits. It is never from God. God gets uncomfortable when you mourn for too long or celebrate your mourning. He sees what you do not see and knows what pertains in the spirit realm. Prolonged mourning draws evil spirits whose work is to keep you in that state of mourning. This they do by ensuring that bad events continue coming your way, so you continue 'celebrating' with these spirits. It is, therefore, not strange that death visits certain areas of the globe too often.

In the spirit world, the enemy toys with death and visits when you stay in a state of mourning for too long. Like little children who are bullied by their superiors who go as far as forcing them to wear tattered and dirty clothes to embarrass them and force them to dance to their tunes, so does the enemy manipulate through a prolonged state of mourning and disappointment. The enemy of your soul is not supposed to toy with you during your bereavement, but you easily play into his hands when you allow him to play with your emotions.

The Spirit of the Lord

A few years ago whilst working as a physician, in the consulting room, I noticed that many of the 'sick' people who came to me were suffering from disappointment, hence, they were in despair. Some were stuck in life because they had lost a boyfriend, husband, or friend. Others could not move on after failing an examination, being rejected, or not appreciated. I allowed God to use me to speak comfort and hope into these lives, and many of these were touched by God's Spirit.

I noticed how people who came in sad, depressed, and despondent left with their spirits lifted. Something started to happen in my own life around this period, although I really did not appreciate what was happening. Patient after patient began telling me how they felt better just talking to me. I noticed this was the working of God's Spirit upon me.

It takes a tangible presence of God to break the back of disappointment, despair, and sorrow. This is because these negative states are enforced by beings unseen to the normal eye who are happy only when you get disappointed. These influences like attention, and they get this attention from innocent and naïve mortals who continue mourning in their disappointment beyond what is healthy.

God's presence drives out the spirit of mourning and despair. The spirit of mourning comes with heaviness, and, together, they put upon you an invisible garment — a spiritual form of ashes, sackcloth, and heaviness. God's Spirit breaks these negative influences and removes their dirty, miserable garb from you. This process takes time, but when He is through with you, you begin to manifest His joy externally. The sure mark that you have been loosed from the bondage of mourning and despair is when God's Spirit of joy manifests with praise from deep within you.

The crippling effect of mourning is no more when your feet are spiritually loosed to dance in joy as you praise God. There are many times you cannot tell why you are glad and so exuberant. You just notice some form of explosive joy from deep within. This can be done by no man; it is the work of God's Spirit. It is the comfort of God's Spirit and not human comfort.

Human comfort operates at the level of the soul and does not truly liberate. It just soothes momentarily — like an emotional masturbation. However, God's comfort is an anointed, empowered comfort that reaches into the depths of your spirit where disappointment holds you bound. It is a yoke-breaking force that truly liberates.

Chapter Nine

> *The Spirit of the Lord GOD is upon me, because the LORD has anointed me to bring good news to the poor; he has sent me to bind up the brokenhearted, to proclaim liberty to the captives, and the opening of the prison to those who are bound; to proclaim the year of the LORD'S favor, and the day of vengeance of our God; to comfort all who mourn in Zion, to give them a beautiful headdress instead of ashes, the oil of gladness instead of mourning, the garment of praise instead of faint spirit; that they may be called oaks of righteousness, the planting of the LORD, that he may be glorified. They shall build up the ancient ruins; they shall raise up the former devastations; they shall repair the ruined cities, the devastations of many generations.*
>
> **Isaiah 61:1-5**

Chapter 10
LIFT UP YOUR DEFENCES

Chapter Ten

Guard Your Thought

> *If you're reading this...*
> *Congratulations, you're alive.*
> *If that's not something to smile about,*
> *then I don't know what is."*
>
> **Chad Sugg**
> *(Monsters Under Your Head)*

Do not listen to all the conversation in your head about how bad life has become. If your meditations are always negative, then most likely evil is their driving force. The presence of evil is a truth, and Satan is the real being behind it and part of the agenda is to torment you, frustrate your life, and keep you stagnated with regret. He loves to torment and see you harassed, depressed, and bound. When he puts sickness, depression, pain and any other yoke upon you, not only does he seek to harass you but to harass all who are with you and care for you.

Satan seeks to cut off all forms of comfort to your ailing situation. This he will do by making those who still love you to feel like you are now becoming a burden. Job's wife, who was supposed to give him some form of comfort, began to see him as a big burden and wanted to get rid of him. Satan worked in this woman to give voice to exactly what Satan desired from Job: to denounce God and his love.

> *So Satan went out from the presence of the LORD and struck Job with loathsome sores from the sole of his foot to the crown of his head. And he took a piece of broken pottery with which to scrape himself while he sat in the ashes. Then his wife said to him, "Do you still hold fast your integrity? Curse God and die."*

Job 2:7-9

Satan afflicted Job's body, his mind, and his soul. He was so grievously stricken with sores from the crown of his head to the soles of his feet that he could not fathom what was happening to him. His mind was so troubled he could not put the sudden, puzzling outcome of his health together mentally. Psychologically, his wife did not help matters, for she added to his misery by asking him to curse his God who had forsaken him and then die. His body was hurting; his soul was harassed not just with his predicament but with the apparent lack of comfort from his wife. His spirit man was under severe spiritual pressure. He felt an absence of God and His love.

Job's theology of God, His love, and His care was turned upside down. His understanding of the causation of disease evaporated and blew out the window. He was left standing emotionally, psychologically, and physically alone. Overnight, Job found himself 'alone' on a platform of great spiritual vulnerability. His integrity was under serious attack!

Do Not Isolate Yourself

> *"I realize, for the first time, how very lonely I've been in the arena. How comforting the presence of another human being can be."*
> **Suzanne Collins**
> *(The Hunger Games)*

In killing your joy, Satan would work to isolate you from God, from your family and friends, from your loved ones and their comfort. In the throes of your pain, you still need God even when it appears He has forsaken you. You need to believe that God still cares, and this is important for you to feel the love of God, His embrace, His care, and His provision. You will also need the comfort and company of friends and family. Without them, the pains of the storm get to you. Company is soothing; company brings healing, and that is why Job's friends came to sit with him immediately when they heard about his predicament.

> *Now when Job's three friends heard of all this evil that had come upon him, they came each from his own place, Eliphaz the Temanite, Bildad the Shuhite, and Zophar the Naamathite. They made an appointment together to come show him sympathy and comfort him. And when they saw him from a distance, they did not recognize him. And they raised their voices and wept, and they sat with him on the ground seven days and seven nights, and no one spoke a word to him, for they saw that his suffering was very great.*
> **Job 2:11-13**

Some storms of life cannot be stopped but only endured. You need the company of good people who will not barrage you with useless questions and suggestions. When life is difficult, you need a companion to hold your hand and tell you that it shall be well. Difficult and distressing paths are always better walked with a known hand clutching yours. Many times in one's life's journey, companionship will prove priceless.

"And as ridiculous as it may sound, sometimes all any of us needs in life is for someone to hold our hand and walk next to us."

James J. Frey
(The Final Testament of the Holy Bible)

I love some aspects of the African culture where family and friends just come to sit around those who are bereaved or are going through tragic moments. Sitting with a friend or neighbor or even going along with a friend to visit someone you do not know and console the person is a great thing to do.

Do not permit the enemy to keep you bound, separated, and caved. He seeks to make you crazy and wretched like the madman of Gadara (Luke 8). This madman dwelt in the tombs with the dead. He was isolated from family and friends. Satan tormented him day and night and kept him bound. When Jesus healed him from all the harassing demons that tormented him, Jesus sent him back to his family and to his people.

> *Return to your home...*
> **Luke 8:39**

It Is Okay to Speak Out

When you are hurt, cry out, scream, and, sometimes, even shout. Pouring out your sorrow is fine, and it does bring some form of healing. Those who bottle up all their pain hardly ever move into true healing. People pour out their sentiments, fears, disappointments, and anger when they are wounded. It is not surprising that, in the midst of this, you will say things you are not supposed to say and ask all forms of questions. It is part of the healing process, hence, do not feel bad about it. Many times, you ask 'What if?' and 'Why was this or that not done?' You ask all these to appease yourself that, maybe, you could have averted the present predicament. Job did the same when he found himself struck by a very strange disease.

"Why did I not die at birth, come out from the womb and expire? Why did the knees receive me? Or why the breasts, that I should nurse? For then I would have slept; then I would have been at rest, with kings and counselors of the earth who rebuilt ruins for themselves, or with princes who had gold, who filled their houses with silver. Or why was I not hidden [as a] stillborn child, as infants who never see the light?

> *Why is light given to him who is in misery, and life to the bitter in soul, who long for death, but it comes not, and dig for it more than for hidden treasures...*
>
> **Job 3:11-16, 20-21**

Do Not Nurse Your Anger

There is a place to cry out and pour out the anger within you, but if anger is nursed for too long, it becomes poison that leads eventually to self-destruction. Vexation has a way of poisoning your soul and spirit. It blinds you to every good thing around you, and you begin to see all things in shades of 'black'. Everything and everybody becomes a problem, and soon you begin to find fault with people.

> *Surely vexation kills the fool...*
>
> **Job 5:2**

Anger at others and at God harbored for a long period of time opens you up to demonic control and manipulation. Like blood from a fresh wound attracts sharks to potential prey, so does a wounded, bleeding soul attract demonic attention.

> *Be angry and do not sin; do not let the sun go down on your anger,
> and give no opportunity to the devil.*
> **Ephesians 4:26-27**

> *Refrain from anger, and forsake wrath!
> Fret not yourself; it tends only to evil.*
> **Psalm 37:8**

If you focus on your pain, you open yourself up for more pain. However, if you focus on the positive, even in the state of despair, you will draw the strength of God to help you with your situation.

Do Not Encourage Satan's Accusations

There is an accuser who seeks to harm you at all times. It is a voice that seeks to keep you down, depressed, and subdued. In the heat of your suffering, you can easily fall prey to the manipulations of the evil one. He uses the power of voice, speaking directly to your soul in order to steal your peace. There is often a kind of rationalization fueled by the enemies of your soul. Do not allow such rationalizations to continue, or your entire psyche will slowly warm up to these negative voices. There will be voices telling you all kinds of negative things, but you need to make a conscious effort and surround yourself with positive things and positive voices.

Do not let the enemy tell you that 'the darkness' in your life is a result of the wrong things you have done. You may begin to blame yourself for the misfortune. Do not work yourself into a pity party or hang a noose around your neck. People around you, too, may not help with their thesis on the laws of cause and effects. You may see God as the One reproving you. God is not wounding you; neither is He shattering your life. No matter what you have done, what sin you have committed, God loves you, and He seeks to forgive you, heal you, and comfort you.

Even if you are responsible for the problems you are facing presently, God is willing and able to forgive you and restore you.

> *He will deliver you from six troubles; in seven no evil shall touch you. In famine he will redeem you from death, and in war from the power of the sword. You shall be hidden from the lash of the tongue, and shall not fear destruction when it comes. At destruction and famine you shall laugh, and shall not fear the beasts of the earth.*
> **Job 5:19-22**

It is important rather to reflect on God's word and on His love. It is His love that will heal your broken heart and mend your wounded soul.

God Has Not Done It!

You need to connect to the right source of all goodness — God. You can bet on a good God. Anytime you walk truthfully with God and trouble knocks on your door, God is not to blame. Deep trouble can destabilize you so badly that your very foundations of faith will be shaken. Weak faith will not stand against strong storms. In the midst of thick darkness, even the faithful can doubt the goodness of a good God. Indeed, this is the very intention for the enemy's attack on your health, your job, your relationships, your mind, your emotions, and your peace.

The devil wants you to doubt the existence of God, and, just in case he fails to dissuade you, he will want to paint God black and engage you in an unvoiced discourse that will end with your putting the blame for all the pain and hurt you are going through at the doorsteps of God.

It is natural to blame God when you find yourself in the furnace of unending trouble. Of course, you expected Him to shield you from the stormy blast and not to hand you over to the schemes of your enemies. So when trouble hits repeatedly and your resolve to stand wanes, you easily shift the blame from the enemy to God. This perception is in your mind even though you may not openly voice it. When the arrows of pain and frustration upset your normal and peaceful life, when your peace is smashed and your health messed up, human reason, with help from the accuser, will directly put the blame at the doorstep of God even though it may not be so. Job went through the same valley, and it is not surprising that he blamed God.

For the arrows of the Almighty are in me; my spirit drinks their poison; the terrors of God are arrayed against me.
Job 6:4

Do Not Wish Death for Yourself

In the throes of trouble, it is easier to see yourself as so disadvantaged that it appears that there is more hope for the inanimate than there is for you. Gloom and doom obscure vision and foresight. Once you are alive, there is nothing like impossibility. God can reverse negative trends. He can turn misfortune into great fortune. Remember that, even for a tree, when it is cut down and its shoot burnt, as long as its root remains in the earth with the stump, it has hope. At the scent of water, the stump will bud again, with branches shooting out (Job 14:7-9).

Death and mourning often whisper in the valley of the shadow of death. This results in thoughts of death. You envisage all things drying up and all good things dwindling. Do not entertain thoughts of death or mourning beckoning you to the land of the dead. Refuse to see doom and blackness, and do not dance to the dirge the enemy sings at your door. The mountains may break apart and may be uprooted from their familiar abode. The age-old rocks may wear out with time and disappear, yet you must refuse to allow your predicament to cast down your countenance.

Do not let death and its whisperings bring your spirit so low that you prefer death to life. Fill your mind with the truth that God is your refuge and strength. The unprecedented may occur, and the unthinkable may come to pass, yet, if you stay close to God in the face of the deepest darkness, joy will keep death and mourning at bay. God is your refuge and indeed your strength. He will be there by your side when you face trouble. The sons of Korah in ancient Israel composed a song that testifies to the above. It is found in Psalms 46:1-7:

> *God is our refuge and strength, a very present help in trouble. Therefore we will not fear though the earth gives way, though the mountains be moved into the heart of the sea, though the mountains tremble at its swelling. There is a river whose streams make glad the city of God, the holy habitation of the Most High. God is in the midst of her; she shall not be moved; God will help her when morning dawns. The nations rage, the Kingdoms totter; he utters his voice, the earth melts. The LORD of hosts is with us; the God of Jacob is our fortress.*

If you will learn to nurse the joy of the Lord by putting a helmet of God's love and protection over your head, fear and death will flee. With fear and death kept at bay, the kingdoms that stood against you will begin to totter. A heavenly host of angels and the commander-in-chief Himself — Jehovah — will step in to lead you out of the valley of the shadow of death.

You may have a great destiny, but fear and death can rob you of it if you permit them. The God of Jacob is the God who defends those pursued by fear and death. When Jacob the son of Isaac 'stole' Esau's blessing and he sought to kill him, Jacob's life was preserved by the God of Jacob despite his faults and mistakes (Genesis 27:41-41). When Laban decided to cheat Jacob time and again, the God of Jacob continued to bless him and preserved his life.

The Holy Spirit is the Spirit that gives joy and strength against fear and death. The more joy you have, the more death loses its power over you. Mourning draws death closer, but joy draws life closer and pushes death away. With the joy of the Lord in place, God will jump unto the battle front, and every battle or war you find yourself in will lose its control over you.

The bows and the spear of death sent to slay you are pulverized. All sophisticated ammunition of hell against you will burn by fire. This is why, in Acts 9:40, when Tabitha died, Peter had to drive away the mourners before God could use him to raise her from death. In Matthew 9:23-25, when the ruler's daughter died, Jesus had to drive away the dirge flute players and the mourning crowd before He could revive her.

If you stop listening to the whisperings of fear, death, and mourning, you will rest in peace, and you will know the joy and deliverance in the presence of your God. There, indeed, is a fortress in God for all who believe and know how to hide in it. It takes sticking close to God and blocking your ears and heart to fear and all evil forebodings in order to drive death far from you. This is because the Holy Spirit is activated by faith and not fear.

If you believe in God's covering and strength, you directly harness the shield of faith, which quenches all fiery darts of fear and death. Then you activate God's power of deliverance and covering through the Holy Spirit, and He becomes a terror to all who seek to drown you.

> *Come, behold the works of the LORD, how he has brought desolations on the earth. He makes wars cease to the end of the earth; he breaks the bow and shatters the spear; he burns the chariots with fire. "Be still, and know that I am God. I will be exalted among the nations, I will be exalted in the earth!" The LORD of hosts is with us; the God of Jacob is our fortress (Emphasis mine).*
>
> **Psalm 46:8-11**

Fear can never cohabit with joy. Anytime you embrace fear, you directly push joy away. Fear comes with anxiety and ill will. When the storms of misfortune hit you, watch closely, for fear and anxiety often trail it. Every battle with trouble has to deal with anxiety and fear, too. If you do not deal with the fear and the anxiety brought by this current storm, your healing will delay. Fear also is tied to death and the foreboding of death. When you are

Lift Up Your Defences

trudging through the valley of foreboding, you will need faith in God that things will get better.

The winds of positive change can come your way again, but you need to hold onto hope — hope that God can help you put your family together. You need to believe that the wayward child will be restored. Your business can turn around, and the infirmity in your flesh can be healed. The years you lost to betrayal and disloyalty can be restored by the healing grace of God. Pain, misfortune, and fear can kill the force of love and take soundness from you. Do not grant trouble the opportunity to hurt you further.

Even though everything around you may not be working as you want, this is not your end. Things may appear to be dying all around you, but you will not die. God will keep you and protect you as you go through this deep and dreary valley. The shadows all around you may be dark and fearsome, but you have what it takes to beat them. May the light of hope and God's comfort meet you as you look to Him.

God will walk with you, no matter how long it takes to get you out safely to the borders of the land of hope and prosperity. If only you permit God, He will restore your joy and grant you His Spirit of love and soundness of mind. You need to believe that, even in your present predicament, there is a good God who knows what you have been through. He has kept you alive to this moment, and He will continue to watch over you. He will help you put food on your table, and your children will not go hungry. You will find rest again. You will find comfort and peace again. God will help you get restoration in your soul.

You may be confused and not know what steps to take. You may be very bitter presently from your hurt and wish to be mean to those who offended you. Walking in offence will not help restore healing and joy to you. May God help you to take the right decisions and respond rightly. This misfortune will work for your good. You will come up at a higher level and celebrate your victory over the storm. After God restores you, you will forever be sure of the fact that His goodness and mercy will not leave you. May you come out stronger on the other side as you determine to respond positively.

Remain Calm for the Battle Ahead

Anybody who is born of a woman has some days that are full of evil. The truth is that you are always engaged in one fight or another. The problems of life may seek to drown you, but you need a calm spirit to keep your head up. You need to cultivate inner rest and stability even whilst all hell is breaking loose around you. If you do not have inner rest, you will not have the strength to combat the pressures that seek to drown you.

When you remain calm, your spiritual eyes shift from focusing on the negative to the positive. You begin to see an access route out of your present predicament. Your eyes are fixed on the ancient foundations and on the Lord God, the Maker of heavens and the earth. You will then begin to appreciate the Maker of heaven and earth that He is still on the throne. Your foot will not be moved (Psalm 121:1-3).

Your ability to deal with forces beyond your natural strength depends on your ability to keep your eyes, faith, and confidence fixated on God and His ability and willingness to protect you. If you concentrate on the gloominess of your situation, you will not find the strength of God.

> *For it is you who light my lamp; the LORD my God lightens my darkness.*
> **Psalm 18:28**

If your focus remains on God, He infuses your inner being with His supernatural strength to deal with difficult situations. You will leap over unseen walls and even go through barricades. You will begin to run supernaturally, like the cheetah. You will harness the endurance of the camel and the strength of the ox.

> *For by you I can run against a troop, and by my God, I can leap over a wall.*
> **Psalm 18:29**

What controls the activities, plans, and schedules of men in the natural world will lose control over you. All machinations of hell and the underworld will fail in their attempt to keep you down. God will become a shield to you as you take refuge in Him. Your feet will then be strengthened as those of the wild deer. The force of God will enter into your arms, and your arms will bend a bow of bronze. You can then pursue your enemies, and those who rose up against you will sink. You will beat them to dust, and the wind of God will drive them away. Even cosmic forces will not be able to harm you.

> *The sun shall not strike you by day, nor the moon by night.*
> *The LORD will keep you from all evil; he will keep your life.*
> *The LORD will keep your going out and your coming in*
> *from this time forth and forevermore.*
>
> **Psalm 121:6-8**

Chapter 11
GOD IS JUDGE

Only God Knows Your Pain

God will fight for you! For everything man does under the sun, there will be a day of reckoning. Whatever you sow, you will surely reap. If you believe this, you will understand why you need to leave all judgment to God. It is very difficult to let go when others have spitefully used or despised you. The desire to hit back, even in a small way, is innate. You need to choose to walk in love even when you have been hurt.

The Bible admonishes you to hate what is evil and love what is genuine. Evil and good are not defined by what is acceptable and practiced by many but by what the word of God spells out. The truth never changes, and time, civilization, and sophistication cannot alter it. Sin has corrupted your human nature and blinded you to God's word, which is truth. If you choose to do what all offended people normally do, you will end up in a pit.

> *... And if the blind lead the blind, both will fall into a pit.*
> **Matthew 15:14**

You are entreated to love one another with brotherly affection and, as much as possible, to live at peace with all men. How can you do this all the time, even to the point of having love for those who have consciously hurt you? Truly, it is *difficult* to walk in love and be a genuine Christian. Christianity is a very long and tiresome journey — full of temptation, being despised, being ridiculed, and even being shamed. Yet you forget that you have surrendered your will and future to Him who knows best and who sent His Son to ransom you from eternal destruction.

If you expect God to take you where He has planned for you, then you need to obey His instructions in detail. You will get to your destination only if you keep close to your guide. God's word is a lamp unto your feet and a light to your path. In obedience to God's word, try your best to bless those who have hurt you.

Bless those who persecute you; bless and do not curse them.
Romans 12:14

Only God Knows the Pain You Have Been Through

Life's problems were not meant to be carried alone. God, in His infinite wisdom, made you a social being and has enabled you to be there for others in their moments of trial. However, in the thick storms of life, even your social networks might fail you. God sits enthroned in the heavens, observing the dealings of men. Nothing escapes His scrutiny. When you are tossing in your sleep, He knows, and He sees. When you cry, He is aware of every tear that falls from your eyes.

> *You have kept count of my tossings; put my tears in your bottle. Are they not in your book?*
> **Psalm 56:8**

God knows your frame, indeed, and He has not forgotten that you are dust. He created you, and He knows you are like grass, hence, your glory does not last. His steadfast love for you abides forever. He knows your past, present, and future and has redeemed you from the pit of this misfortune and crowned you with steadfast love and mercy. You may be feeling down and out, depressed, broken, and battered. You may feel forsaken and betrayed, yet God has not forsaken you. He knows what you have been through and all who have wounded you.

A nursing mother may forget her suckling infant, but your Maker will not do that. You are too dear to Him to be forsaken or ignored. God knows all the hurt others have dished into your lap, and He cares for you.

> *But Zion said, "The LORD has forsaken me; my Lord has forgotten me."*
>
> *Can a woman forget her nursing child, that she should have no compassion on the son of her womb? Even these may forget, yet I will not forget you. Behold I have engraved you on the palms of my hands; your walls are continually before me.*
> **Isaiah 49:14-16**

In your pain you should still hang onto hope. Hope will keep you alive. It takes a lot of courage and hope to still believe that God is on your side when your physical body is ravaged by diseases that seem difficult to cure. Ravaging disease can cause your breath to be abhorrent to your wife. Your own children may come to see you as a bother and your siblings consider you a nuisance. All your good friends may forsake you, and your servants may even treat you as a stranger. Your paths may look dark and dreary, and you may even wish for death to come for you sooner than it should. Job found himself in such a situation, and he could not fathom what had gone wrong. Yet amazingly, he still clung to hope. Without hope, you are as good as dead. All is not lost. This is the way to go. Your Redeemer lives, and He will show up for you in the end. May you find strength to continue to push on. It is surely not over, and, until you give up, help is coming!

Oh that my words were written!
Oh that they were inscribed in a book!
Oh that with an iron pen and lead
they were engraved in the rock forever!
For I know that my redeemer lives,
And at the last he will stand upon the earth.

Job 19:23-25

Where there is life, there is hope. Your sun will shine again. This is not your end! Watch over your heart, let nothing kill or steal your joy. When your joy is gone, your strength to fight on is gone. May God's power and presence continue to keep and uphold you. May you survive every storm and may your head be lifted up. Surely there is hope for the righteous and your expectation will never be cut short. Keep believing, and keep moving on, this phase too shall pass.

God bless and keep you.

www.ingramcontent.com/pod-product-compliance
Lightning Source LLC
Chambersburg PA
CBHW061444040426
42450CB00007B/1203